Life cycle support in the Ada® environment

Life cycle support in the Ada environment

JOHN McDERMID
Systems Designers Ltd, Fleet

KNUT RIPKEN
TECSI - Software, Paris

The right of the
University of Cambridge
to print and sell
all manner of books
was granted by
Henry VIII in 1534.
The University has printed
and published continuously
since 1584.

Published on behalf of
the Commission of the European Communities by
CAMBRIDGE UNIVERSITY PRESS
Cambridge
London New York New Rochelle
Melbourne Sydney

Published by the Press Syndicate of the University of Cambridge
The Pitt Building, Trumpington Street, Cambridge CB2 1RP
32 East 57th Street, New York, NY 10022, USA
296 Beaconsfield Parade, Middle Park, Melbourne 3206, Australia

First published 1984

Printed in Great Britain at the University Press, Cambridge

Library of Congress catalogue card number: 83-18911

British Library cataloguing in publication data
McDermid, John
Life cycle support in the Ada environment.
1. Ada (Computer program language)
2. Computer programs
I. Title   II. Ripken, Knut
001.64'24   QA76.73.A35

ISBN 0 521 26042 6

Contents

Contents

Contributors

This book is derived from the final technical report of a study performed by Systems Designers Limited, and TECSI - Software. The two main contributors to this study, and the two main authors of this book, were John McDermid and Knut Ripken, however a large number of people contributed to the study and hence indirectly to the production of this book.

Important contributions to the study were made by J P Keller, G P Mullery and N V Stenning. Managerial support, contributions in discussions, and constructive criticism during the study were received from J P Doutriaux, J Favaro, J P Levy, D Llewellyn, J M Sezerat, M Stokking, R G Sutherland and I C Wesley.

Valuable information for the book was gathered on a visit to the USA. The main contributors were Th Cheatham Jr, C Heitmeyer, J J Horning, D C Luckham, J McClean, S Owicki, D L Parnas, E Satterthwaite, E Schmidt, A I Wasserman and D Weiss.

Useful comments on the study reports were given by C Bjoerkvall, M Czerwinski, B T Denvir, A J Dignan, B Dion, K Katzoff, P Kornerup, J M Maestracci, D Monaco, E Ploedereder and M Sintzoff.

This book could not have been produced without the support of the Commission of the European Communities. We are pleased to be able to acknowledge the support of the Commission, and, in particular, the assistance given by H Hunke and R Meijer, during the study, and to M W Rogers who arranged for the publication of the book.

We offer our thanks to all the contributors to the

study, and we offer our apologies to anyone whose contributions
we may inadvertently have forgotten to mention.   We do, of
course, accept responsibility for any errors and omissions
which there may be in the book.

JAMcD, KR

1
Introduction

1.1 Background

This book results from a study entitled "Life Cycle Support in the Ada Environment" which was performed between January and October 1982 by Systems Designers Limited and TECSI-Software. The study was performed with the sponsorship of the Commission of the European Communities under their Multi-Annual Data Processing Programme.

1.2 Scope of the book

The scope of the book is the methods, tools and database facilities needed to provide support to the whole life-cycle of large scale software systems written in Ada. Although the focus is on Ada as the target programming language few of the methods and tools studied are influenced by the characteristics of Ada. In particular almost all of the management methods are independent of Ada. Thus the book has considerable relevance to the production of software in languages other than Ada.

The book also focuses on the development of embedded systems, but again this bias has comparatively little impact on the generality of the discussion of methods and tools.

The methods investigated provide guidelines for software development, maintenance, and management. The aim when selecting methods for investigation was to produce a coherent methodology which would assist in the cost-effective production of reliable systems which could be shown to satisfy their requirements. Thus the emphasis was on existing methods which had been shown to be of practical value in the production of large systems.

The purpose of a tool is to support a method by automating some aspect of the use or application of the method. This book distinguishes different levels of tool support. A minimal set of tools would give clerical support to the methods by recording in a database the information produced by using the methods. A more advanced set of tools would automate the production or checking of this information according to the rules defined by the methods.

In Ada parlance the set of tools plus the underlying database facility is known as an Ada Programming Support Environment, or APSE. The APSE concept was described in the Stoneman Report published by the US DoD in February 1980 [Department of Defense (1980b)].

Stoneman advocated a phased bottom-up approach to APSE development in which an initial basic environment termed a MAPSE could subsequently be extended to produce a range of APSEs offering progressively more powerful and better integrated support. As a consequence, Stoneman concentrated on the requirements for an APSE foundation in terms of a Kernel and Minimal APSE (KAPSE and MAPSE), and only briefly considered development and management methods and the tools required in a full APSE.

In contrast this book clearly tackles the requirements for, and the choice of, methods and tools for a full APSE. It concentrates on the combination of methods for software development, integration, maintenance, and configuration control, with those for project management, to produce a coherent software development and maintenance methodology. Once a coherent methodology has been produced it is possible to see how the methods can be supported by tools to form an APSE giving <u>coherent support for the whole software life-cycle</u>.

Throughout this book emphasis is placed on the coherence of methods. The idea of a coherent methodology was outlined in a report, usually referred to as "Methodman", which was published by the US DoD [Department of Defense (1982b)] after the main technical work described in this book had been completed. Methodman is more limited in scope than this book as it only considers development methods. However, as far as the requirements for methods and tools are concerned Methodman and this book are largely in agreement.

Methodman concludes that a number of coherent software development methodologies exist, although none of them adequately cover the entire software life-cycle. This conclusion also appears in earlier comparative studies of methods, e.g. that performed by the Augusta Consortium [Augusta (1981)], and was forcibly brought home to us in discussions with acknowledged experts in the field of software engineering. Consequently this book treats coherence and complete life-cycle coverage as issues of central importance. This book goes beyond Methodman by describing a particular instance of a coherent methodology, and by giving an assessment of the individual methods based on the experimental use of the methodology. The book also describes the tools and database facilities which would be necessary to support this methodology, so it presents a description of a coherent APSE.

This description must be seen as illustrative, not definitive, as it describes an APSE which could be built, but not necessarily the best which could be built using existing technology. Further the description of methods and tools concentrates on development and management methods, and to some extent neglects validation and testing methods. Also, the investigation of tools has taken a rather secondary role as a consequence of the belief - also espoused by Methodman - that tools can not properly be considered until a methodology has been established. This unevenness of coverage within the book reflects resource limitations in the performance of the study rather than unresolved technical problems.

It seems clear that development of an (Ada) programming support environment which even begins to meet the ambitious objectives that have been identified for them, e.g. by Wasserman et al [Wasserman (1981a)], will be a major

undertaking. It is also evident that many workers in a
variety of fields have a valuable contribution to make, and
that truly successful programming support environment
developments will demand extensive communication and
collaboration between these workers.

Therefore this book only represents a small step
towards the production of a coherent APSE, but we believe
that it is a valuable step as it contributes to the
understanding of the characteristics of a coherent APSE,
supporting the whole software life-cycle. It is intended
that this book should provide a basis for further
collaboration and discussion. This book should therefore be
treated in the same spirit as Stoneman and Methodman, that
is, used as a <u>reference point for further work on APSE
design and development</u>.

1.3 Contents of the book

The main part of the book summarises the results
of the study, and some corroborating detail is presented in
the annexes. The experimental work of the study is not
detailed here, but it is recorded in a series of reports
[Systems Designers Limited (1982a-h)].

Section 2.1 introduces the generic life-cycle
model which we developed for the study, and which underpins
the rest of our work. The model identifies the levels of
representation produced in developing a system, and the
transformation and validation activities which occur during
the software life-cycle. Section 2.2 considers the overall
requirements for a coherent APSE, and, in particular,
considers the characteristics required of the development
and management activities in order that they may properly be
integrated. Section 2.2 ends with a discussion of criteria
by which the methods may be assessed. Section 2.3 introduces
the instantiation of the life-cycle model which defines the
methodology which we have investigated in detail. Section
2.4 outlines the requirements for the individual methods
which comprise the methodology defined in section 2.3.

Section 3.1 gives a more detailed description of

the development methods which we have employed, and
indicates how well these methods meet the requirements and
criteria established for their assessment. Section 3.1 also
indicates alternative methods which are applicable within
our model, and which would have to be considered in an
exercise looking for the best currently available methods to
apply to the development of Ada programs. Section 3.2
provides a similar set of descriptions and analyses for the
management methods.

For a reader who only wishes to gain an overview
of the methods it is probabaly satisfactory to miss out
sections 3.1 and 3.2 as the methods are described in outline
in chapter 2.

Sections 3.1 and 3.2 give an essentially static
description of the methods. Section 3.3 describes the checks
which have to be made in order to validate the accuracy of
the development process, and the effects of making a change
in the requirements for the system, thereby giving a dynamic
description of the methods. Section 3.4 considers the tools
which could be produced for use within an APSE in order to
support some set of methods. This section tries to identify
a generally useful set of tools, rather than just being
confined to tools for supporting the methods discussed in
detail earlier in the book.

Chapter 4 presents the conclusions from our
study. Section 4.1 considers the value and generality of the
conclusions which we are able to make on the basis of our
comparatively brief study. Section 4.2 describes the
benefits which we believe will accrue from the use of a
coherent APSE, and section 4.3 discusses the technical
limitations of an APSE based on the methods which we have
investigated in detail. Section 4.4 discusses development
plans for a coherent APSE, and thus addresses the technical
feasibility and cost of producing an APSE. In section 4.5 we
outline a course of action which we believe would lead to
the production, acceptance and use of a "medium-scale APSE"
by the software industry.

The Annexes contain the corroborating detail and

some useful ancillary material. For example Annex 1 contains
extracts from the reports describing the use of the methods
[Systems Designers Limited (1982a-h)], and Annex 5 is a
glossary written so that it can   be used either for
reference, or read as an introduction to the terminology of
programming support environments for those unfamiliar with
the subject.

2

Requirements for, and choice of, a coherent APSE

2.1 The Life Cycle Model

The Life Cycle Model adopted by this study is based upon recognition of the need to employ multiple levels of abstraction in the development and maintenance of a software system. During the development process several distinct representations are produced, one at each level of abstraction.

The highest level of explicit representation must state the requirements for the system. It should reflect the overall function of the complete embedded system and the environment in which it is to operate. This representation must give the complete picture, without obscuring the description of what the system does with irrelevant details. At the lowest level there must be a "representation" which actually "does the job" - that is the actual program or suite of programs. At this level the concern is very much with how the system operates.

It is assumed that the gap between these two levels is so great that it can not conveniently or reliably be bridged in a single step, hence several intermediate representations will be required. This leads to a sequence of representations as shown in Figure 2.1.

Development proceeds from the highest level representation to the lowest level. It must therefore be possible to transform each representation to produce its successor in the sequence. The term "transform" is used in the broad sense of an operation which takes a representation as its input and produces another representation as its output. Note that the transformation might involve taking

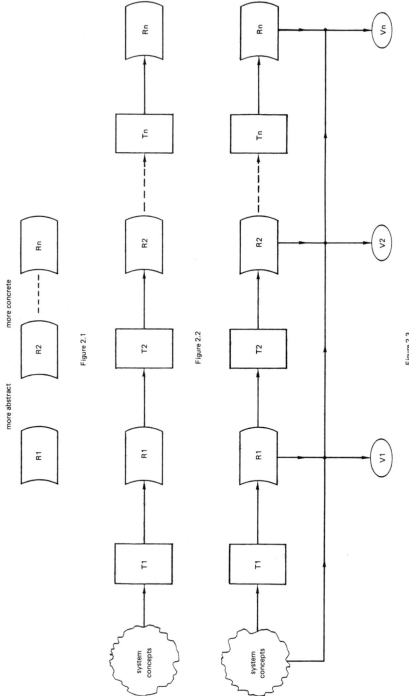

more abstract

more concrete

R1   R2   Rn

Figure 2.1

system concepts — T1 — R1 — T2 — R2 — Tn — Rn

Figure 2.2

system concepts — T1 — R1 — T2 — R2 — Tn — Rn
V1   V2   Vn

Figure 2.3

design decisions so the output representation may not be isomorphic with the input representation. Also note that the transformation may be based on information taken from more than one representation.

In general information may be gained and lost during a transformation. Transformations between representations are shown in Figure 2.2. The "System Concepts" in this picture can be viewed as an implicit representation of the system in the minds of those people who are responsible for the systems procurement and use.

For an orderly development process it must be possible to verify each representation as it is produced (where the term "verify" is used to mean "increase confidence that the representation is satisfactory for its purpose"). In practice it is useful to distinguish two kinds of verification:

1 within a representation: verification that a given representation is internally consistent and logically complete;

2 between representations: verification that a given representation is consistent with the earlier representations in the sequence.

Both kinds of verification are reflected in Figure 2.3. This figure also shows that verification may involve reference to any of the "earlier" representations in the sequence, not just the immediate predecessor. Note that informal verification of the lowest level of representation (the working system) continues for as long as the system is operational.

Unfortunately it must now be recognised that in reality the development of complex systems does not proceed in the straightforward fashion suggested by Figure 2.3. Attempts to develop and verify later representations will lead to the identification of errors and misguided design decisions which influenced the production of earlier

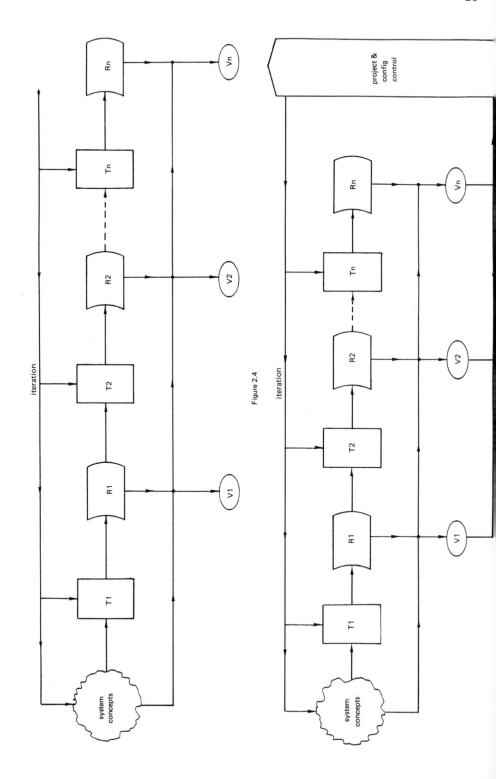

Figure 2.4

representations. Further, as the system and its environment become better understood so the requirements imposed on the system are likely to change.

In either case there will be a need for iteration around the representations as shown in Figure 2.4. On each iteration some existing representation will be changed to correct the detected error, or to reflect the change in requirements, and the changed representation will again be verified. These changes will be carried through to all later representations, and these will also be re-verified. The model recognises both the fine and coarse iteration and imposes no bounds on the number of iterations which can occur.

The model does not regard the representations as being monolithic, and it recognises that the production of one representation may start before the previous one is complete. This, coupled with the presence of iteration in the model, means that the model encompasses the incremental development of software, or stepwise refinement, as it is sometimes known.

The general model of the development process is now almost complete. However the presence of iteration leads to non - trivial problems in retaining control of the overall process, and these are compounded by the fact that there is often a need to develop several distinct versions of a given system. Thus there is a need for effective project and configuration control to which all development activities must be subject. Incorporation of these controls leads to the complete model as shown in Figure 2.5.

There are a number of project management functions implicit within the configuration control box in the model. Project management is responsible for planning and controlling the development and maintenance processes which will lead to the production and modification of the representations. Some of the representations, for example the module code, will comprise a large number of related components, rather than being one monolithic object. Thus integration management, that is the collection and combination of the components into coherent products, is also implicit in the configuration control box in the model.

Clearly the model does not show all the details of the development and management processes. Nonetheless it provides a framework for the investigation of software development and, to a lesser extent, project management methods. Major characteristics of a given method that can be explored with the aid of the model include:

1   the level and purpose of the various representations that are employed;

2   the form and notation used for each representation;

3   the means of performing the transformation from each representation to the next;

4   the way in which each representation is validated;

5   the means by which iteration and change propagation are controlled;

6   the overall approach to configuration control.

Because alternative development methods can differ significantly in the manner and purpose of representations that they employ, the representations in Figure 2.5 have deliberately been left uninterpreted. However, in order to provide a more concrete illustration, Figure 2.6 gives a generic indication of the levels of representation which might be employed by a "complete" software development method.

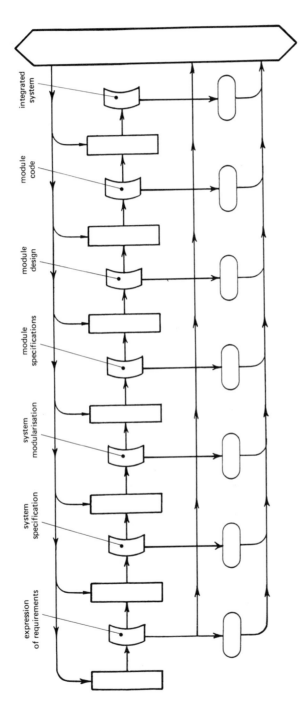

expression
of requirements

system
specification

system
modularisation

module
specifications

module
design

module
code

integrated
system

Figure 2.6   A possible set of representations

2.2 Overall Requirements for a Coherent APSE

2.2.1 Development Methods

A Development Method is concerned with one or more levels of representation within the Life Cycle Model. We can view any Development Method as comprising three major components, viz:

Notation   - the notation in which the representation is expressed;

Guidelines - guidelines for producing the representation;

Analyses   - rules for checking the internal consistency and completeness of the representation and for checking its consistency with respect to the representations from which it was derived.

Clearly the Guidelines govern the Transformations in the Life Cycle Model, and the Analyses define the Verification activities in the Model.

The notations are a major factor governing the coherency, or otherwise, of the APSE. If we are to produce a coherent APSE, from the point of view of the Development Methods, then we require that the representations of each method allow us to show the relationships between each representation. This means that the methods must be based on one, or a compatible set of, system models. Additionally the representations must be capable of being held within the same database. More significantly we require the notations to be such that the Analyses, including those for checking consistency between representations, can be automated, or at least machine assisted. This latter requirement is particularly constraining on the combination of methods which can be used in an APSE.

The Development Methods must cover the whole spectrum of the Life Cycle from initial capturing of requirements to the production and release of complete software systems, and the maintenance and enhancement of systems after the initial product release. For a coherent APSE there should be no gaps or conflicts between any of the Development Methods. In other words there should not be any part of the transformation process which is not addressed by one of the methods, nor should any part of the transformation be addressed by more than one method (in incompatible ways). Similarly each verification activity must be uniquely defined. This can be summarised by saying that there must be a smooth transition between "adjacent" methods.

In order to have coherency with the Management Methods the representations used by each Development Method must be amenable to the chosen method of Configuration Control. This constrains the granularity of the objects, and the relationships between the objects, in the representations. Similarly the Transformations and Analyses must fit into the model of system development encompassed by the Project Mangement Method.

We briefly describe the chosen Levels of Representation in section 2.3, and give a more detailed account of the requirements for the methods associated with each of these levels in section 2.4 together with a justification for our choice. A description of our chosen methods is given in section 3.1.

2.2.2   Management Methods
2.2.2.1   Introduction

An APSE for the development and maintenance of fully engineered embedded systems has to provide substantial management support as well as development support.

The characteristics of embedded systems e.g. large size, long life, continuous adaptation to changing requirements and customisation necessitate the effective management of dynamically changing system structures and organisational structures. As Lehman [Lehman 81] puts it: "A programming manager's principal function is, in a very general sense, the management of evolutionary change".

2.2.2.2 The Scope of Management Methods

Management support has to cover economic and organisational as well as technical tasks concerning the whole spectrum of the life-cycle. Economic and organisational tasks are:

1 Planning and organisation.

2 Progress monitoring.

3 Control by taking corrective action.

Technical tasks are:

1 Definition of versions and releases.

2 Establishment of Project Standards.

3 Technical coordination of:

   3.1 internal deliveries and integration.

   3.2 simultaneous development, maintenance and regeneration or redelivery of several versions of several systems.

4 Introduction of new tools.

2.2.2.3 Effectiveness of the Management Methods

To be effective, management must keep system and organisational structures in harmony. To justify this point we quote from Lehman [Lehman 81]. Although Lehman recognises that "it is generally accepted that the structure of at least one major operating system was a direct reflection of the organisation that created it" and that "that system's structure was undoubtably a major contributing factor to the very high cost and the major difficulties encountered in its subsequent maintenance" he maintains that "in any event, in a large project is may be profitable to maintain and relate models of the system and organisational structures". He claims that "their usage and support constitutes a potentially rewarding technology that must be explored in the context of Programming Support Environment design".

In this sense, to be effective, management has to assign appropriate work packages to appropriately skilled groups of people. Consequently it is advantageous to distinguish life cycle phases which reflect different types of work.

As well as ensuring that the appropriate skills are applied to each phase of the development, the use of different teams gives us a basis for controlling the quality of the representations produced. If one team performed the whole development it would be quite easy for valuable information to remain unrecorded in the database, with consequent problems when it comes to maintenance. If, instead, separate teams are used, and the team which has to use a representation is responsible for checking its completeness before accepting it from the team who produced it, then it is much less likely that any information will remain unrecorded.

If we divide the life cycle into, say, specification, design, coding, integration and maintenance phases, then the representation produced by the design team should contain sufficient information to allow the coding team to perform their job, and similarly for the other phases. We summarise this by saying that the representations produced at the end of each phase should be "sufficient" representations. In practice it is unlikely that the representations produced will be sufficient. Nonetheless the ideal of sufficiency is a good metric against which to judge the quality of a representation, particularly one produced at the end of a phase.

2.2.3 Configuration Control
2.2.3.1 Introduction

Development and management methods both require a powerful underlying method for configuration control.

This book views development as a sequence of transformation activities each leading to a new representational model of the system to be developed. The degree of human involvement in the transformations may vary from nil, to 100%. Management methods apply both to the human and machine based activities. The management methods rely on the representations produced (the results of the activities) as a basis for monitoring and controlling project progress.

Since the results of the activities (documents, sources, reports, objects, subsystems, test plans etc.) will be in constant evolution due to iteration between the levels of representation, they will exist in multiple versions. Thus it is essential for an APSE to possess a method for keeping tight control over all the data being created and used so that costly inconsistencies can be avoided.

Such a method may be implemented by a configuration control system which can be seen as a subsystem providing an interface between a data base and the development and management subsystems, as illustrated in Figure 2.7.

Configuration control is crucial to the success of large scale software development and maintenance. Industry has become gradually aware of the important role of configuration control, influenced by the experience of hardware configuration control. Researchers in software engineering, however, have not paid much attention to Configuration Control. Even a recent article by W E Howden [Howden (1982)] fails to deal with the issue. We have attempted in this study to overcome this deficiency by paying particular attention to configuration control issues.

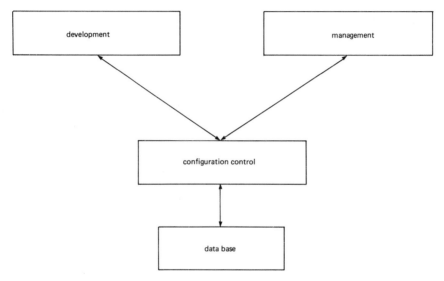

Figure 2.7   Configuration control system interfaces

2.2.3.2 Macroscopic and Microscopic views of Data

In an APSE many different representations for
systems, subsystems and modules may be produced at different
stages. All these representations, whether they are texts,
sources, object binaries, test data, test results,
management reports, etc., will be called documents in this
book.

Thus documents are the primary results of life
cycle activities and are data of "large grain size". Many
APSE activities could be performed more effectively and
naturally if they manipulated data of smaller grain size,
i.e. data contained within documents.

Consider, for instance, an Ada source: the whole
source text constitutes a larger grain than, say, a context
specification or a type definition within the program unit
defined by the source text. Ideally there should be APSE
methods defined for zooming in on, say, a type definition in
order to examine its relationship with an abstract type
definition (as a small grained data item contained in a
higher level document) or in order to change it. We
summarise this by saying that, ideally, an APSE should
permit microscopic views of representations and microscopic
operations upon them.

An example of a Programming Support Environment
which permits microscopic views is the Harvard-PDS developed
by Cheatham et al [Cheatham (1981)]. In the Harvard-PDS a
document is called a "module" and an enclosed data item is
called an "entity". We prefer to call the enclosed data
items of small grain size "atomic data items". This should
not, however, mislead the reader to believe that atomic data
items exist only on one semantic level. In general there
will be a hierarchy of atomic data items in any
representation.

Further we believe it to be helpful to describe
a document as having:

1   an ergonomic,

2   a syntactic, and

3   a semantic

dimension. The ergonomic dimension corresponds to the way
the document is manipulated by a user or a tool (a source
text is, for instance, the object which is edited). The
syntactic dimension corresponds to the structure of the
document (an Ada source has the syntactic structure of an
Ada programming unit, for example) and leads to the
identification of data items of smaller grain size which are
part of the document. Finally, the semantic dimension
corresponds to the semantic relationships involving
documents and data items.

        The atomic data items are thus syntactically
identified and there may be arbitrarily complex semantic
relationships between these data items. If we are to support
microscopic and macroscopic views of the representations
then the Configuration Control system must be able to
maintain the consistency of relationships between atomic
data items as well as between documents.

        As a consequence of the requirement for
microscopic views documents must have a well-defined
structure. This indicates that even informal documents
should be structured at least into a set of potentially
nested textual or graphical items with which justification
and/or comments may be associated.

2.2.4   The Database

        Stoneman [Department of Defense (1980b)]
promoted the idea of the database as the central element of
the environment serving as the container of all the
information relevant to projects over their whole life
cycle.

        If an APSE is to permit and exploit microscopic

views of documents then it is not adequate to think of the database in terms of its implementation on top of a hierarchical file system. Instead it is appropriate to describe the data base with an entity-relationship model (or a derivative model). This point of view is taken by Olivetti on the Danish-Italian CEC-sponsored MAPSE development as well as by the UK Ada Study Group.

2.2.5   Assessment Criteria
2.2.5.1   Criteria for the Individual Methods
The following have been identified as desirable characteristics of methods, and therefore provide criteria by which possible methods can be assessed. Some of the criteria are quite general, but a number of them clearly apply only to the development methods.

Practicality

A method must provide practical assistance on real projects. Methods which cannot readily be applied to large scale systems should be avoided. Further, methods which are very rigid - for example those which insist that a particular specification must be expressed completely within some formal language - may present more problems than they solve, and hence should be avoided. A method which cannot yet readily be applied, but which could become readily applied if supported by appropriate tools could migrate from being impractical to being practical in the sense defined here. The size of system which can be handled with the currently available tool support is a rough metric of the practicality of a particular method.

Ease of Use

A method should be accessible to a reasonably competetent designer or programmer. A method should ideally be easy to learn, and easy to apply once learnt, although ease of initial learning is clearly the least important of these two criteria. Ease of use will often be difficult to assess as it depends to a considerable degree on the level

of tool support available for the method, and the training
of the people using the method.   However if a method is
highly effective it will be worthwhile providing the tools
and training necessary to enable the method to be used
easily. The productivity when using the method and the cost
of providing the tools and training are rough metrics for
ease of use.

Formality

a well defined set of rules of how to do it.

Formal methods are preferable to those which are
ad hoc or which only give general guidelines. Formal methods
give a way of achieving the precise system descriptions
necessary for producing a reliable system which can be shown
to meet its requirements. Clearly these first three criteria
are closely related and formality must be balanced against
the two criteria above, in order that practical, usable,
methods emerge. A metric for formality is difficult to
define. Perhaps the best metric is the extent to which the
notations have a sound mathematical foundation.

Also it must be accepted that completely formal
treatment of non-trivial systems is not yet feasible -
consider for example the current capability of program
proving systems. However formal methods can be applied in
several areas, and even where a complete formal treatment is
not feasible it may still be useful to treat parts of a
system formally. For example key parts of a program may be
selected for formal verification.

Finally it must be recognised that investigation
of formal methods has a major beneficial influence on more
pragmatic techniques, and that a general knowledge of formal
methods results in better programs even where the methods
themselves are not extensively employed.

internal checking consistency and completeness

Verifiability

It should be possible to verify or validate the
products of a method so that there can be a high degree of
confidence that these products meet their requirements.
Methods with a formal basis are more likely to offer the

possibility of complete verification than would be feasible
with informal methods. An ideal metric for verifiability
would be the degree of confidence which could be obtained in
the correctness of a representation produced by a particular
method, once the verification had been performed. A less
precise, but more practical, metric is the richness of
semantic checks which can be performed on the representation
by the verification activity.

Incremental Analysis

           With certain approaches to program development
the only identifiable "product" is the complete program.
Such methods offer little hope for achieving good management
control over software development as it is very difficult to
assess progress. On the other hand methods which permit
frequent and incremental analysis give a good basis for
monitoring and hence controlling technical progress. A rough
metric for this criterion is the granularity of
representation on which analysis can be performed.

Ease of Change *change with narrow impact*

           An associated criterion is the ease with which
changes to representations can be handled. Clearly methods
which do allow a representation to be produced and analysed,
or verified, incrementally are likely to be much better able
to handle changes than those which have a monolithic view of
systems. Ease of change is difficult to quantify but a rough
metric would be inversely related to the amount of
unnecessary consequent change or reverification which has to
be made after a particular change has been made.

Tool Support

           It is possible to envisage some level of tool
support for almost any method. However a method for which
strong tool support could be provided is obviously
preferable, for APSE purposes, to one for which only minimal
support could be offered. Conversely a method which demands
excessive tool support before its use can be contemplated is

likely to involve high risk as it does not offer an
evolutionary path to a coherent APSE through manual
application of the method. Twin metrics would be the maximum
level of tool support which could practically be provided
and the minimal level of tools necessary so that a method
can be used.

Standard Components

Ideally a method should provide a framework in
which it is feasible to employ libraries of standard
components. This applies at the level of specifications as
well as at that of the operational program components. This
criterion is essentially a binary one, although it may be
easier to use standard components with some methods rather
than others. In practice the phase of the life cycle will
probably affect reusability as much as the properties of the
individual methods.

2.2.5.2   Criteria for Combination of Methods

The above criteria apply to individual methods.
There are certain criteria however which apply to the
combination of methods employed within an APSE.

Life Cycle Coverage

The combination of methods should offer full
coverage of the software life cycle. In particular they
should recognise that a project does not end as soon as the
system is installed and begins operation. Changes are
inevitable and the methods should therefore make provision
for iteration and change propagation, and ensure that
overall control of the products and of the development can
still be retained. A metric for life cycle coverage would
have to take into account:

1   the number of life cycle phases supported;

2   the number of notations that were defined;

3   the number of the transformation and verification
    activities   for   which   guidelines   and rules are
    defined.

Such   a   metric   would clearly be rather more vague than the
above list implies.

Combination of Methods

The   combination   of   methods   should   not   only
provide   good   support   for   each individual activity in the
Life   Cycle,   but   should also provide for smooth transition
between   the activities (and methods).   Ideally there should
be   no gaps, clashes, overlaps, or difficult transformations
needed   in   carrying   the results of one activity forward to
the next. Also we   require that it be easy to verify that one
representation   satisfactorily   implements   the semantics of
the previous representation.

This criterion is clearly   related to Life Cycle
coverage, but is more complex in   that   clashes   have   to be
catered for. It would be assessed as being inversely related
to the number of transformations   for   which   no   guidelines
were   supplied,   and   the   number   of   inter-representation
verifications   for which no rules were supplied.   Additional
factors would be the number of representations or activities
for   which   more   than   one   notation   or   set   of rules was
defined.

It   is   desirable that one representation of the
system   produced   by   one   method   allows   "natural"
representations   of   the   system   to   be   produced   by   the
subsequent   methods.   By   "natural"   we   mean   that   a
representation can be seen as conforming   to   good practices
for producing that representation (using that notation), and
that the style of the representation is similar to the style
which might have resulted had the   notation been used alone,
rather than as part of a coherent methodology.

This quality is important   because   an unnatural
style of representation will probably be hard to understand,

and may even be unintelligible without reference to the preceeding representations. It is desirable that most representations be understandable on their own, and this property is essential for the end of phase representations to be "sufficient", as defined in section 2.2.2.3.

It is very hard to quantify "naturalness" although it will usually be quite clear when unnatural representations have been produced. It may help, however, to give examples of unnatural representations. Ada programs which were produced using only arrays, and not the other type facilities, would (almost indubitably) be unnatural. Similarly representations produced in the predicate calculus, containing universal quantifiers but not containing existential quantifiers, would (almost indubitably) be unnatural.

Support for all Roles

The combination of methods must provide support for management, as well as technical development, activities. Ideally the combination of methods should provide some form of support for such activities as estimating, feasibility analysis and complexity measurement.

A metric for this criterion would be based on the number of roles supported, compared with the number of roles identified in the model of the software life cycle.

2.3 Chosen Interpretation of the Life Cycle Model

2.3.1 Introduction

The chosen interpretation of the Life Cycle Model defines the Levels of Representation which must be produced by the Development Methods, and the Management Methods which must be employed. Our chosen interpretation for the Development Methods is illustrated in Figure 2.8.

We describe our chosen Levels of Representation in terms of the development of a System for a Customer. We briefly describe the representation, the transformation and the verification which constitute the method at each level. At each level the verification includes checks that the representation is internally consistent and complete. These checks will not be explicitly mentioned in the ensuing description.

The choice of the Levels of Representation is not an unconstrained decision. In fact it is very strongly influenced by the set of methods available. This being the case we defer justification of our choice to section 2.4 where we describe the requirements for the chosen Levels of Representation in detail.

The choice of the number of Levels of Representation is, to some extent, governed by the size of the system to be produced. In general the larger the system the more levels are required in order to master the complexity of the system, particularly in the area of system design. We describe below what we believe to be the minimum number of distinct representations given our chosen methods, but recognise that there may be multiple levels of description within any one representation.

The configuration control box in the model encompasses all the Management Activities, and not just configuration control. Seen as the head of the development cycle it represents the management functions of organising and controlling the development activities. Seen as the tail of the the cycle it represents the management function of progress monitoring and the configuration control functions of identifying and recording data produced by the

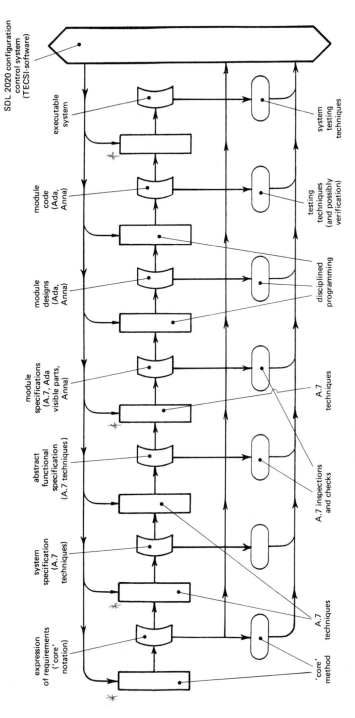

Figure 2.8   The chosen interpretation of the life cycle model

development methods, and of maintaining data consistency.

Despite the fact that the management functions are not made explicit in the Life Cycle Model shown in Figure 2.8, they are of central importance. This is particularly so because they are involved in controlling or monitoring every transformation or verification activity which occurs during the development and maintenance of a product.

We will consider the Development Methods first, then describe the Management Methods.

2.3.2 Requirement Expression

The Requirement Expression (RE) representation is a description of the environment in which the system to be developed will work, plus an outline of the intended function of the system. The "transformation" is the process of extracting from the customer his requirements for the system. This will probably involve interviews with the customers representatives, or reading existing documents. It may be necessary to reconcile conflicts between differing views among the customers representatives. The verification involves checking by the customer that the representation accurately describes his needs. This is the only practical method of checking the RE so the representation must be capable of being expressed in a way accessible to the customer. Consequently the RE may have to be couched in an informal notation.

2.3.3 System Specification

The System Specification (SS) representation is, in essemce, a "black box" specification of the system behaviour. It must specify the inputs to, and outputs from, the system, and specify the operations which the system performs in deriving the outputs from the inputs. This representation may be much more formal than that in the RE as it is intended for use by the system designer, not by the customer. The transformation therefore consists of re-expressing part of the RE, and adding extra information, as necessary, obtained from further contact with the customer. The verification is concerned with showing that the SS is consistent with the relevant part of the RE.

2.3.4 Abstract Functional Specification

The Abstract Functional Specification (AFS) is the highest level of system design. The representation specifies the functions implemented by the system, the data flows within the system, and the data flows which cross the system boundary. The AFS is very similar to the SS except that it shows internal system structure rather than external behaviour. It is a set of interconnected "black boxes", rather than one "black box". The AFS expresses a language independent (and hardware/software independent) design. The "transformation" is the skilled task of design, and the verification has to show that the AFS correctly implements the SS.

2.3.5 Module Specification

The Module Specification is a high level, programming language oriented, design specification for the system. It states the decomposition of the system into modules, and the functions performed by each module. The notation must show concurrency explicitly at this stage. The transformation is a continuation of the design process, refining the AFS. Verification involves showing that the MS correctly implements the AFS.

2.3.6 Module Design

The Module Design (MD) specifies the internal structure of the Modules, in a programming language oriented notation. Modules may be nested so the MD notation must have at least the expressive power of that for the MS. The transformation is again design refinement, and the verification shows that the representation is a correct implementation of the earlier MS. Modules for testing purposes may be present in the MD.

2.3.7 Module Code

The Module Code (MC) representation comprises the Source Text for the Modules and may additionally contain annotations clarifying the semantics of the Modules. Depending on the size of the system it may not be appropriate to separate the Module Code and Module Design representations. The transformation is the final stage of design refinement, and the verification shows that the MC correctly implements the MD.

2.3.8 The Executable System

The Executable System (ES) must contain code in a suitable form for loading and execution. It may also include symbol tables for debugging, test harnesses, and so on. Run-time support facilities may also be present at this stage, but may not have any counterpart at the previous stages of the model. The transformation will be the automated process of compilation. The primary verification will be largely implicit, in that the syntactic and semantic consistency will be checked by the compiler (which is assumed to be correct). The verification of the transformation will normally be by means of testing, but may occassionally be based on formal verification of the program properties.

2.3.9 Configuration Control

Each life cycle development activity produces a representation of the system to be built. This may be illustrated by a "level slice" through the model as shown in Figure 2.9. In fact, a development activity will generally produce several documents of which one may be the main representation of the system at the corresponding level. The other documents may be indexes, cross-reference listings, internal representations, analysis results, etc. In general the verification activity will also produce several documents. All these documents are defined by the methods employed, i.e. they are part of the data model for the

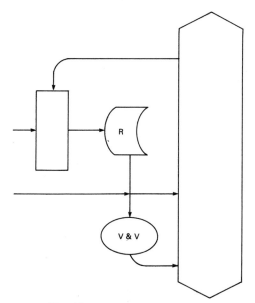

Figure 2.9   A level slice of the life cycle model

system development methods.

By abstracting from the multitude of documents and focussing on the "primary" document of a level, the life cycle model points in the direction of a uniform and generic view of data. This view is necessary for an attempt to define the mechanisms which control the evolution and use of the data produced during the whole life cycle independently of the methods used in generating and exploiting the data.

The life cycle model thus suggests the definition of a generic data model and generic operations for configuration control. The specific documents to be controlled are defined by the development methods. Looking at the big box as a document sink points furthermore in the direction of a "system which never forgets". For such a system, configuration controlled items would not have to be selected manually, instead they are defined by the methods. With such a system, a controlled deletion operation would have to be offered which could eliminate "garbage".

2.3.10 Management

The main management functions always involve planning, project control, staff allocation and organisation within the constraints of the resources (money, people, data, time, ...) available.

The life cycle model hints at the fact that management actions concern the development activities which are performed by people and that they are based upon or aim at their tangible results, i.e. the representations produced or to be produced. The information needed to carry out the management functions appears therefore to be very closely related to the documents kept under configuration control within the data base of the integrated environment - and, especially, with the logical and time dependency relations between these documents. Thus the management functions can be based on the data model which is underlying the configuration control functions.

The sequence of development activities produces a set of documents which are related to each other by their

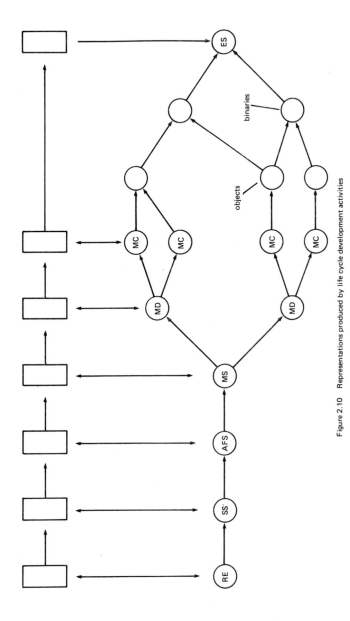

Figure 2.10   Representations produced by life cycle development activities

logical (and temporal) dependencies. An example of the sort
of dependencies which will arise in a typical software
development is illustrated in Figure 2.10.

The overall APSE requirement for keeping system
and organisational structures in harmony (cf 2.2) can be
satisfied by matching the organisational structure with the
system structure (i.e. the above document graph produced by
the overall method) as illustrated in Figure 2.11.

The sets of activities corresponding to
different phases in the life-cycle are assigned to different
teams of people. These sets of activities are delineated by
the broken lines in Figure 2.11. The management team
develops the above organisational structure and assigns the
development of specific representations to the teams whilst
the preceeding activities are in progress.

The assignment of activities in different phases
to different teams is an ideal which serves as a guideline
for project management. In practice resource limitations may
mean that the ideal is not met, and a compromise assignment
has to be made.

The activities of integration are not explicitly
reflected in the life cycle model. They are included in the
configuration management box as technical management
activities.

Since management functions are strongly tied to
the representations being produced, the relevant management
information (deadlines, budget, status etc.) should be
associated with the corresponding representations and should
evolve with them. Further there should be a set of
management representations, or documents, which associate
management responsibilities, methods and data with the
various management teams. These associations can be
controlled by the same configuration management system as
the development representations.

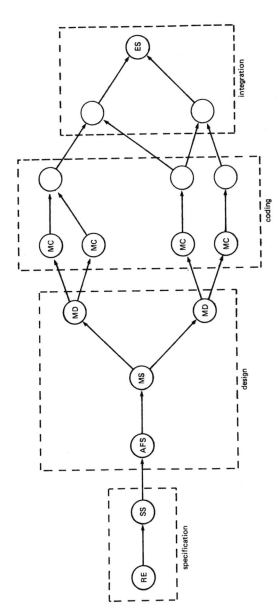

Figure 2.11   Organizational structure

2.4   Requirements for the Development Methods

2.4.1   Introduction

In describing the individual methods we are concerned with three primary properties of each Method.

First we wish to say what information the representation at each particular level should contain, and to outline the constraints on the notation in which it should be expressed.

Second we wish to say how that representation is produced in terms of the transformations which have to be made from the representations of the previous levels.

Third we wish to consider the "local checks" which have to be made in order to ensure that the representation at each level is consistent and complete, and how the accuracy of the transformation between the representations can be validated.

Having chosen our levels of representation and methods it is quite difficult to give genuine requirements for these properties without being unduly influenced by the capabilities of the chosen methods. What we have tried to do therefore is to give an idealised description of the main aims and principles of the methods. This should also allow us to justify our choice of levels of representation before we become concerned with details in section 3.1.

We believe that our methods reflect good current practice and that they are well suited to the development of Ada programs, however, as we pointed out in section 1.2, we can not produce any comparative evidence to show that the methods we have chosen are in some sense "the best".

Choosing Ada as a target programming language and restricting our attention to embedded systems has had an impact on the requirements for the individual development methods. Ada has directly influenced the low-level design descriptions, but it has had little imapct on the other methods and notations. The properties of embedded systems affect the system specification and high level design methods, and the techniques for testing the executable system. These effects are not particularly clear in the

requirements for the individual methods but they do come out
more clearly in chapter 3 where we describe the chosen
methods.

Before we give the requirement for each of the
methods in detail we will consider some aspects of methods
which are pertinent to all Levels of Representation.

2.4.2 Requirements for all Methods

For each method the representation will comprise
logical objects, their attributes, and relationships between
those attributes. Further the methods must combine so that
relationships, e.g. implements/is_implemented_by, can be set
up between the representations of the individual methods.

For any method it may be sensible to structure
the representation into a number of parts, e.g. a full
design specification and a synopsis, or separate description
and justification documents. Consequently the development
method, the configuration control method, and the database
in the APSE, must be capable of supporting a wide variety of
structures for the representations.

The local checks performed for each method are
intended to show that the representation is internally
consistent and logically complete. Logical completeness
requires that for all attributes with which we are concerned
we have made a statement about all values that the attribute
can take, and all the possible conjunctions of these values.
Consistency requires that none of these statements are
incompatible, given the defined relationships. Further
consistency requires that the individual relationships and
the structures which they form conform to some set of
constraints, e.g. that part/ part-of relationships are not
circular.

Verification of the transformation between two
representations requires us to show that the relationships
between the representations are consistent in the above
sense. Further we wish to show that no pertinent information
has been lost in the transformation. The local and
inter-representation checks comprise the overall

verification activity.

Given these summaries of the verification activities we will comment little on verification in the following sections and concentrate primarily on the representation and transformation. We also concentrate on the methods addressing the earlier stages in the development process as these are generally the least well understood, and they are the least constrained by the choice of Ada as the implementation language.

2.4.3 Requirement Expression
2.4.3.1 Aim

The essential function of this Development Method is to extract from the customer for the system enough information to produce an Expression of Requirements for the system to be built which can be agreed on by the customer and the system builder.

The quality of the Requirements Expression (RE) is of extreme importance as it affects the quality of all the other representations, and the amount of iteration which will be necessary in producing the system. Thus we must aim to make the RE as consistent and complete as possible in order to minimise the development and maintenance cost for the system.

2.4.3.2 Overview and Justification

One of the primary difficulties of establishing a Requirement Expression is that the customer (almost inevitably) will have an incomplete idea of what he requires the system to do. Consequently the analyst will have not only to extract existing information from the customer but also cause new information to be generated.

A second major difficulty is that often no individual will understand all the aspects of the system necessary to enable it to be unambiguously specified and produced. Thus part of the Requirements Expression exercise involves distilling a coherent system view from a set of potentially incompatible partial views of the system.

In many cases the customer for the system will
not be a computer expert so the Requirements Expression must
be couched in non computer-specific terminology if it is to
be checked by the customer. Since checking by the customer,
in the widest sense, is the only possible means by which we
can decide whether or not the system we have specified meets
his needs it is essential that the Requirement Expression be
understandable without specialised knowledge of computers.

Thus the primary justification for having the RE
Level of Representation is that it forms a basis for an
agreement between the system builder and his customer about
what the customer wishes to have built. The RE is thus of
benefit both to the system builder and the customer.

Whilst it is probably adequate to express the
requirements for the computer system per se for the purpose
of developing the system, it is necessary that the
environment in which the system will operate be understood
so that these requirements can be produced in the first
place. Since any changes in the environment may impact the
function of the system it is sensible to retain a
representation of the requirements expression for the
environment, as well as the system, within an APSE. This
provides justification for the RE being concerned with the
systems environment as well as the system itself.

2.4.3.3 Representation

The Requirements Expression (RE) contains
descriptions of the data objects in the environment, the
functions in the environment, and the functions performed by
the system. It also describes the usage of the data objects
by the functions.

Strictly the RE should not state how functions
are broken down within the system. In practice it will
probably be necessary to describe a (possible) high level
design of the system in order to convey to the customer the
intended function of the system.

It is not clear what level of detail, or
precision, is appropriate to the RE. Our experience however

indicates that it may be necessary, in order to retain ease
of communication with the customer, to accept an RE which
contains some ambiguity, and which does not specify in
complete detail all the desired system functions. These
shortcomings should be rectified in the System
Specification.

The above discussion indicates that it will be
necessary to produce, or at least present, the RE in an
informal notation. For practical purposes we can assume that
the RE will be couched in an informal notation, at least in
initial APSE developments. In the longer term it may be
possible to produce the RE in a formal language and generate
"natural language" interpretations of the RE for use by the
customer for the system.

Further the form of the RE held in the database
may not be readily accessible to the customer. It may
therefore be necessary to generate a conventional narrative
document (or set thereof) for communication with the
customer.

The RE may contain performance constraints,
reliability requirements, and so on. We believe it to be
very important that this sort of data be expressed
parametrically as it is very unlikely that performance
requirements, for example, will be absolute: they should not
therefore be elevated to the status of being part of the RE,
since the RE may well be quoted in the contract for the
construction of the system.

2.4.3.4 Transformation

The "Transformation" to produce the RE consists
of information gathering and analysis activities.
Information gathering must start first, but the activities
will normally proceed partly in parallel.

Information gathering will consist of
interviewing the customers representatives, reading
narrative requirements documents (or a combination of the
two)· and recording the derived information within the
database. The skill in this process is in trying to ensure

that all the relevant information about the system has been elicited from the various sources, and ensuring that one consistent system view has been produced.

2.4.3.5 Verification
The analysis activity introduced above consists of performing the local and inter-representation checks. The local checks try to ensure that all the information in the RE is compatible. Further they have to show that there are no dangling references, i.e. that information which source A says should be provided by source B is actually provided, and so on.

The check on the transformation consists of getting the RE reviewed by the customer, and obtaining his approval of the RE as representing that which he requires to be built.

2.4.4 System Specification
2.4.4.1 Aim
The aim of the System Specification (SS) is to give an unambiguous and detailed description of the functions which the system should perform and the data flows which cross the system boundary. Ideally the SS should contain enough information to allow the system to be built without further reference to the customer for clarification of his requirement. In other words the SS should be a sufficient representation.

2.4.4.2 Overview and Justification
The System Specification (SS) is produced by restating unambiguously and precisely that part of the RE which describes the system, referring back to the customer for further information where necessary. The SS is essentially a "Black Box" specification which states what data enters and leaves the system, what functions the system performs, but does not state how those functions are performed.

The inclusion of the SS in our chosen Levels of

Representation is necessary primarily because the RE is not sufficiently precise to be used as an input to the design process. The SS is limited in scope to the the system to be built, and its interfaces, as no use would be made of a more precise description of the system's environment.

Making the RE more precise and producing the SS may involve a certain number of design decisions, for example, in specifying the details of the user interfaces to the system. The design and performance constraints associated with the RE should be taken into account when producing the SS and, in particular, when making the above design decisions.

Because of the need for precision the SS will ideally be expressed in a formal notation. We argued above that the RE notation must be informal so we must have separate SS and RE representations rather than making the SS simply a more detailed part of the RE.

2.4.4.3 Representation

The RE identifies the inputs to, and outputs from, the system to be built. The SS defines the structure of, and legal values of, these inputs and outputs. There are many systems whose behaviour depends on an internal record of previous inputs, not just the current inputs to the system, so the SS representation must also define the structure and values of data retained by the system. In theory we could specify the behaviour of the system in terms of the history of inputs to the system. In practice we believe this approach will be very cumbersome, especially where the set of objects stored by the system is a function of this history, and we believe that it is better to specify behaviour in terms of data retained by the system. Clearly specifying retained data items could unduly influence the design and care must be taken to avoid this pitfall. In summary we believe that it is necessary for pragmatic reasons to diverge from the ideal of "pure black box specifications" and to explicitly represent data retained by the system. This point is argued in more detail in [Systems

Designers Limited (1982b)].

The behaviour of the system is defined by specifying it as transfer characteristics of a set of functions existing at a single level. These functions take the system inputs and retained data items as inputs, and generate the system outputs and retained data items as outputs. The SS must also specify the physical sources and destinations of the inputs and outputs in order to properly describe the system interfaces. Since we are concerned with embedded systems the notation needs to be geared towards the description of systems in terms of events and actions, rather than in terms of, say, interfaces and databases which might be appropriate for information systems. The convergence of embedded systems and information systems in certain applications, e.g. Command and Control Systems, may mean that hybrid notations will have to be developed in order to produce satisfactory specifications for these applications.

Our experience indicates that it is useful to separate the description of the system into one part describing the data items and the functions, and a separate part describing the mapping of the data items onto sources and destinations. By separating the description of the system into these largely orthogonal logical and physical parts, the SS is greatly simplified. This is particularly so where there is a one to many relationship between logical and physical objects.

The SS should also contain other useful information for the system designer. For example an indication of likely changes will aid the application of information hiding principles in system design.

2.4.4.4 Transformation

Much of the information presented in the SS is already available in the RE. The tranformation thus consists of re-expressing the relevant part of the RE and expanding it so that it contains all the information necessary to allow the system to be designed and built. This transformation will entail the resolution of ambiguities in the RE, and eliciting further information from the customers representatives. This transformation may involve "design", e.g. in defining dialogues across man - machine interfaces.

Given the RE as a starting point we seem to have little need of guidelines for the transformation. However by following a set of guidelines it is possible to perform a check on the accuracy of the RE and deduce where extra information is necessary. By starting with the outputs from the system, then defining the functions necessary to derive these outputs the set of inputs and retained data items can be defined. This may indicate omissions in the RE, and conversely any additional inputs or retained data items in the RE may indicate omissions from the set of outputs.

2.4.4.5 Verification

The local and inter-representation checks are perfomed as described in section 2.4.2 above. The RE is not as detailed as the SS so the inter-representation check really only shows that the SS is plausible given the RE, not that it is "correct". Since the SS is really a more detailed and precise expression of requirements it is desirable to have it checked by the customer, however this operation will probably be difficult because of the notation in which the SS is couched. This problem can partially be overcome in a number of different ways. For example the SS can be "animated" by having an executable specification language, or by means of fast prototyping. Alternatively a "natural language" version of the SS could be generated from the formal notation in which the SS is couched, assuming that adequate natural language generation techniques can be developed.

2.4.5 Abstract Functional Specification
2.4.5.1 Aim

The aim of the Abstract Functional Specification (AFS) is to give a high level functional design description for the system without making any commitments to implementation strategies, e.g. which functions will be implemented as procedures and which as tasks, etc. Thus the AFS specifies the (chosen set of) functions which the system must perform in order to satisfy the requirement. The AFS should also be independent of hardware issues such as choice of processor, or whether single or multiple processors will be used.

2.4.5.2 Overview and Justification

The AFS is the highest level design description for the system, and, as such, is largely concerned with the logical rather than the physical structure of the system. Both aspects of system design are important, but we believe it sensible to separate them and to describe the logical aspects first for a number of reasons.

First software design is a difficult task and separating logical and physical issues is a useful separation of concerns.

Second many software systems are produced in many versions conforming to the same functional specification, but implemented on different hardware configurations, or with slightly differing modules. It is therefore more efficient to specify the logical and physical structures separately.

Third we are dealing with long-lived systems subject to change both in the logical structure (due to a change in the requirement) and the physical structure (possibly due to a change in the implementation technology). It is simpler to handle these changes if the logical and physical structures are separated.

Finally, regardless of the importance of the physical structure it is not possible to record the physical allocation of functions to processors, for example, before we have specified what functions the system must perform. Logical design must therefore be recorded first.

Having said this it must be recognised that the production of the AFS is driven by a number of factors including:

1   physical structure of the target system;

2   logical functional decompostion;

3   logical data decomposition;

4   assessment of the feasibility of implementing
    particular functions (within given space and time
    constraints);

5   size of the work packages for individual
    programmers.

The method for producing the AFS should be
capable of taking into account all these factors, and giving
the most emphasis to the factor which is most important for
a given application.

In practice this stage is one of the hardest in
any top - down system design, and it is likely that many
versions of the AFS will be produced before the first
working system is delivered.

2.4.5.3   Representation

The Abstract Functional Specification (AFS) is a
very similar representation to the SS, except that it
records actual inputs and outputs, and is concerned with the
internal structure of the system, not just with its
behaviour.

The AFS defines the structure and possible
values of the data entering and leaving the system, and the
data which has to be retained within the system. It also
defines the functions performed by the system and shows how
these functions map onto those defined in the SS. These
functions may form a hierarchy (note that those in the SS
may not) and they may include "common use" functions, i.e.
functions which can be used in the implementation of more
than one other function.

The notation required is very similar to that required for the SS except that facilities are required to show how functions at the higher levels in the hierarchy may be implemented in terms of those lower in the hierarchy.

It is desirable to be able to record different design options at this stage, then to be able to choose a particular design for the implementation of the system. It is also extremely important to record the reasons why particular design decisons were made. This information could prove invaluable during system maintenance.

2.4.5.4 Transformation

The transformation involved is that mystical operation known as design. Ideally we would like a set of guidelines which enable us to produce "good" designs in a number of senses, e.g. easy to understand and modify, efficient, robust, and which take into account the factors identified in section 2.4.5.2 above. Unfortunately nobody appears to understand the design process sufficiently well to produce such a set of guidelines. This problem can be illustrated by considering some of the few guidelines which do exist.

Two guidelines due to Parnas are the well known ideas of Information Hiding and Separation of Concerns. The difficulty in applying these guidelines comes in knowing which information to hide, and which concerns to separate. Whilst some suggestions have been made, e.g. hide information which is likely to change, there does not appear to be an adequate set of guidelines for us to be able to identify a method per se. We have to rely on the skill of the designer to some extent, much as we relied on the skill of the analyst in the requirements stage, and accept that we do not have an adequate set of guidelines for the design process in general, and high level design in particular.

A consequence of this is that there will probably be a fairly low level of tool aid to the transformation process for some time to come. However the tools and the database in the APSE must allow the designer

easily to develop, experiment with, and modify designs
because of the essentially iterative nature of the design
process. If the facilities provided discourage the designer
from experimenting within the APSE, then it is likely that
important design information may remain unrecorded, and this
may lead to problems in maintenance. Thus "support" for the
transformation primarily means not unduly constraining the
creative design processes.

2.4.5.5 Verification

Our main local checks again are for consistency
and completeness.

The check on the transformation is more complex
in that we wish to show that the design as expressed in the
AFS implements the requirements expressed in the SS. The AFS
contains an explicit record of the relationship between the
SS functions, and the AFS functions. We can use this
relationship together with the definition of the AFS
functions to show the conformity of the design to the
requirement.

2.4.6 Module Specification
2.4.6.1 Terminology

In describing the Module Specification we use
the term module to mean an Ada compilation unit, although
typically it will be a package specification. Similarly we
use the term function to stand for Ada subprograms, tasks
and task entries. The use of the term function should not be
confused with the language construct of the same name.

2.4.6.2 Aim

The aim of the Module Specification is to define
the allocation of functions to modules and to specify the
transfer characteristics of the functions in a precise,
programming language oriented, notation. This specification
should contain enough information to allow the modules to be
implemented without reference to the earlier design
documents. The module specification should also specify how

the functions it contains implement the functions identified
in the AFS, in order to show how the design is being
refined, and to allow the transformation to be checked.

At this stage there may also be some attempt to
perform system sizing operations, and to make a preliminary
choice of hardware. Additionally the mapping of modules etc.
onto the target hardware could be indicated at this stage,
and will have to be specified before system load time. We
have not considered hardware aspects of the development
process in the study so we will not discuss them further in
this document. We note, however, that a number of existing
software products do enable these mappings to be specified.

If we were concerned with producing an
Integrated System Development Environment, rather than a
Programming Support Environment, we would also require a
hardware design notation at this stage in the design
process. Again we will not elaborate on this point as it is
outside the scope of this document.

2.4.6.3 Overview and Justification

The Module Specification (MS) reflects related
design decisions regarding what information should be hidden
in a module, which functions should be grouped into a
module, and how big a module should be in order to represent
a practical unit of implementation.

Since we now wish to show the implementation
strategy for the system in Ada language terms a separate
notation from that used for the AFS is required, and hence a
separate representation is required.

2.4.6.4 Representation

The representation at this level must show how
the AFS functionality will be realised in programming
language terms. It must also show the mapping between the
functions in the AFS and the functions in the MS. This will
not necessarily be a one to one mapping: for example, we may
have to implement more than one version of a function
providing terminal access if we expect to have to support

more that one type of terminal.

The MS must give a precise specification of the semantics of each function in each module, and of the visible data objects in each module. It must also make clear the interaction between the modules in order that the validity of the MS as an implementation of the AFS can be checked. This means that we not only have to specify the uses relationships between the modules, but also the calling relationships between the functions, and the usage of data objects. Clearly the notation is strongly influenced by the syntax and semantics of Ada and, in practice, the notation will include Ada package specifications, etc.

It would be desirable to include with the MS a document or set thereof describing design decisions, and a design overview document such as a Module Decomposition, which would outline the breakdown of the system into major software modules. It is particularly important to record the design decisions which are made in order to satisfy particular implementation constraints, e.g. memory utilisation and response times, as these are likely to be the most difficult decisions to trace later in the development.

2.4.6.5 Transformation

The transformation between the AFS and the MS involves a considerable number of design decisions, concerning the data objects to be used in the program(s), task structures, and so on. Again we do not know of a method which satisfactorily covers this particular transformation. We regard the tenets of Structured or Disciplined Programming simply as guidelines on good practice like information hiding and separation of concerns. One important aspect of the transformation however is the choice of the task structure for the program(s). There are two primary criteria which we must apply.

First the functions in the AFS are implicitly regarded as atomic, that is they appear indivisible to other functions at the same or higher levels in the system. We

must organise the tasks and their entries so that the
implementation of these AFS functions preserves these
atomicity properties.

Second we must consider efficiency in choosing
our task size, and the level of the interface (the size and
nature of the objects passed) between these tasks. This
implies a good understanding of the likely execution
behaviour of the program. Rules for producing good task
structures would be an important aspect of any method aimed
at this part of the Software Life Cycle.

2.4.6.6 Verification

Local checks conform to our general rules. The
inter-representation checks should show that the
implementation specified in the MS conforms to the behaviour
specified in the AFS. This inter-representation check will
involve showing that the chosen representations for the data
objects in the system adequately represent the logical form
specified in the AFS, and that the operations performed on
these objects have the required semantics. In practice this
will probably involve showing that some (low level) data
model implements the abstract properties required for the
AFS data items. This may be quite difficult (even
informally), especially if the representations for the AFS
and MS employ significantly different notations.

2.4.7 Module Design
2.4.7.1 Aim

The aim of the Module Design (MD) is to show how
the Modules should be implemented to satisfy the
specifications in the MS so that they will be efficient,
easy to maintain, and so on. Because of the hierarchical
nature of Ada compilation units the Module Design process
may yield a more detailed module breakdown than shown in the
MS. If this is the case then it is a management decision
whether these additional modules are elevated to the MS, or
remain embedded in the MD.

2.4.7.2 Overview and Justification

Ideally the MD should cut down the implementation options inherent in the MS so that the module programmer is left with a fairly straightforward task, with little scope for producing a wildly inefficient or obscure program. However if the MD is overconstraining then the programming task is likely to be tedious and error prone, hence defeating the object of the MD. Consequently for small modules it may be appropriate to produce Module Code directly from the Module Specification, or to combine the production of the Module Design and Module Code. However for complex modules the MD should provide an invaluable guide to the implementor, and a useful intermediate representation in the process of verifying the Module Code against the Module Specification.

2.4.7.3 Representation

This Development Method is concerned with the design of the internal structure of the individual modules. Here we are constrained to an Ada oriented design language, which will allow us to define the module structure in terms of the subprograms used, the types and data objects implemented, and so on. Since Ada packages (included in the modules in our terminology) may contain other packages, it is necessary that similar statements can be made in the Module Design about these inner modules, as were made in the MS about the outer level modules. Given this requirement, and Ada as a common factor, it seems sensible that the same notation, viz. Ada plus some annotation, be used for the MS and MD.

2.4.7.4 Transformation

The transformation is one of elaborating a high level design into a more detailed one which contains enough information to allow the individual modules to be implemented without (much) further design activity. This process requires less skill than the earlier design stages, and again we can only suggest the principles of structured and discplined programming, rather than indicate a proper method.

It is not practicable to specify the level of detail to which this design stage should go in general. Clearly this must depend on the application, the skill of the programming personnel etc. In practice we may wish to have a number of levels of module design, particularly if the system to be produced is large and complex.

2.4.7.5 Verification

The local checks and interstage checks are for consistency and completeness as usual. We will wish to show the equivalence of the annotations in the MD with those in the MS.

2.4.8 Module Code
2.4.8.1 Introduction

The final two levels of representation are clearly essential, and are well enough understood for us to omit a discussion of aims and a justification for including the representations in our model.

2.4.8.2 Representation

The Module Code (MC) contains the source code of the modules which will comprise the executable system and optionally will contain annotations clarifying the semantics of the modules.

2.4.8.3 Transformation

The production of the Module Code (MC) should be comparatively straightforward given the detailed MD produced previously.

The transformation is the conventional coding process, but working from a far clearer and more precise specification than is normally available.

2.4.8.4 Verification

The checks will be the same as those between the MD and MS and the tools required will be the same.

It is possible, in principle, to perform formal proofs of correctness of the Module Code against the Module Specification. Formal verification is difficult so there is a severe limit on the size and complexity of systems which can be treated in a fully formal manner. Because formal verification is difficult it is also costly, so it is unlikely that there will be many systems for which the cost of formal verification will be justified.

In practice it is likely that formal verification will only be used to prove important properties such as security or safety for systems of critical importance. Ada itself also presents a problem as it is unlikely that the language as defined is verifiable. Thus it may be necessary to produce a subset of Ada for verification purposes. In practice less rigorous verification will give an adequate level of confidence in the correctness of the implementation for many apllications.

2.4.9 Executable System
2.4.9.1 Representation

The representation here will be in some form of object code suitable for link-loading, and may contain code which is derived from a library and is not therefore represented within the Module Code.

2.4.9.2 Transformation

The transformation is performed by an Ada compiler, other compilers or assemblers if more than one language is used, and possibly a linker and loader.

2.4.9.3 Verification

Part of the verification is implicit and is performed by the compiler, link loader etc. However the major part of the verification will normally be performed by means of testing the executable system or parts thereof.

The testing of the executable system is strongly influenced by the fact that we are interested in embedded systems. Few embedded systems can be used for software development, so a number of tools, e.g. PERSPECTIVE [Systems Designers Limited (1983)], now employ a host - target approach to software development. Consequently it is necessary to be able to perform testing in a number of stages, starting with testing individual modules in a simulated environment in the host, and ending with testing the complete system in the target. Thus a range of methods and facilities, from test harness generation and envionment simulation, to down - line loading and debugging, are required for testing the executable system.

Testing, whether purely manual or machine assisted, is a time consuming and complex task. A detailed discussion of testing is beyond the scope of this document, however we will briefly return to this topic when we consider tools in section 3.4.2, and when we consider system integration in sections 2.5.1 and 3.2.2.

2.5   Mangement Methods

2.5.1 Project management

The study produced a characterisation of a demanding project and an undemanding project to define the range of sizes of projects which the study would address, and to serve as guidelines for establishing the requirements for management methods. This characterisation is reproduced opposite in Table 2.1.

The requirements for project management are stated here for demanding projects. For undemanding projects, the requirements are basically the same, however management may take "short-cuts" in several ways, e.g.:

1   suppression of specific life cycle activities.

2   suppression of management levels.

3   concentration of management tasks of different nature in one work package.

Project management covers a wide range of activities and is concerned with several project phases at any given time. The work for the future phases has to be planned and organised on the basis of the existing system representations and their analysis. Progress of the development work in the current phases has to be monitored, evaluated and controlled by taking corrective action. The quality of the system representations has to be controlled throughout the life of a project.

These management activities may be grouped under the headings:

1   Project Planning and Organisation.

2   Project Control.

3   Integration and Quality Management

CRITERIA	THE UNDEMANDING PROJECT	THE DEMANDING PROJECT
Type of Application	Embedded	Embedded
Size of Application (lines of source code)	< 2500	> 50000
Complexity of application system	Low	High
Total number of modules during life of system	< 50	> 1000
Life expectancy of system	< 10 years	30 years
Reliability requirement	High	Very High
Issued to many sites?	No	Yes
Issued in many versions?	Serially (single site)	Concurrently (many sites)
Configuration of host hardware	Centralised/ local network	Highly distributed
Configuration of target hardware	Single Processor	Highly distributed
Maximum size of development team	3	> 100
Experience within development team	2-5 years 65% < 2 years 35%	> 9 years 10% 5-9 years 30% 2-5 years 30% < 2 years 30%
Development team geographically distributed	No	Yes
Motivation within development team	Good	May need support

Table 2.1 Characterisation of project types

These topics are considered in more detail in
the following sections.

2.5.1.1 Project Planning and Organisation

According to the overall requirements (cf
section 2.2), the basis for the planning and organisation of
future project phases is the set of method-dependent system
representations produced so far. The effort required in the
future can be projected on the basis of these
representations. Project planning and organisation falls
into five main activities:

1 Work Breakdown
   The work has to be broken down into packages each
   of which should consist of several tasks. The
   primary criteria for this decomposition are that
   the size and the complexity of the resultant work
   packages and tasks should be suitable for
   assignment to teams and persons, respectively.
   Other criteria are the logical dependencies among
   the tasks and specific organisational constraints
   (e.g. peoples skills, existing teams, different
   development sites).

2 Effort Estimation
   There should be methods which assist in
   estimating the effort needed to accomplish the
   tasks identified in the work breakdown structure.
   These methods should also help to characterise
   tasks as to their complexity and the skills
   required.

3 Work Load Planning
   All the resources available and necessary have to
   be identified. Resources are mainly people but
   also the environment in which they work (office
   and computer equipment, testing software and

hardware etc.).

These resources have to be allocated to the work packages in a work load plan in accordance with the effort estimation and the general project planning.

It should be possible to evaluate the effects of different allocation strategies on the cost and the plan or schedule of the project.

4 Organisational Breakdown

As the basis of the work load planning, personal assignments have to be made, and all the necessary interactions between people have to be organised. Interactions arise, for instance, when one team depends on the work of another team or when two teams both use a particular product. It must be possible to manage the access rights of teams and individuals to specific documents, and it must be possible to define communication paths along which specific documents may "travel" in specific cases.

It should be possible to make dependencies among people clearly visible to all the people involved in order to foster the acceptance of a plan and to establish their commitment to work accordingly.

A specific organisational breakdown is described below in the section on integration and quality management.

5 Iteration of the planning process

The planning process as described above starts by considering the system representations from which the work packages for a future project phase can be derived.

It should be possible to iterate the planning process by reconsidering the work breakdown, effort estimation, work load planning and

organisation breakdown until an "optimal"
satisfaction of all the constraints (resources,
costs, deadlines) is obtained. This process may
even suggest a decomposition of the whole system
to be developed into subsystems with a "global
use hierarchy" and influence the project
objectives in the sense that it may be decided to
aim at a minimal useful system as the first part
of the system to be developed [Hester et al
(1981)]. The reason for doing this is that in
most cases it will be better to deliver a useful
subset of a system in a timely fashion than to
deliver nothing at all.

2.5.1.2 Project Control

The project control activity has to measure and
to evaluate the progress of the work being done in the
current project phase. If any deviations from the plan
(deadlines, budget, resources allocated etc.) are noticed or
can be anticipated, this activity has to take corrective
actions which re-establish complete management control of
the project. Thus project control can be divided into two
main activities:

1 Progress Monitoring

Management needs various kinds of accounting data
for evaluating the progress. Most of this data
should be collected automatically so that the
administrative chores of "creative" development
people are kept to a minimum. The data should be
available in the form of reports which show
deviations from the expected data, viz:

- document status report

- time and effort statistics

- test progress report

- resource deviation report

In order to choose appropriate corrective actions where necessary there should be methods for projecting the effect of deviation trends into the future and for estimating the impact of planning and organisational changes.

2   Corrective Actions
Corrective actions have to be taken by management if they are necessary for maintaining deadlines, budgets, resource allocations, productivity standards, and product quality. There is a whole scale of actions from light to heavy corrections depending on whether they change:

- the resources

- the development methods

- the organisation

- the plan

- the project objectives

- the total project plan

There should be methods which assist in assessing the impact of any corrective action envisaged.

2.5.1.3   Integration and Quality Management
On large projects, a new management level should intervene between the management level concerned with planning, organisation and control and the development

level. The corresponding activity is much more technical:
it's main role is the management of the integration of
various system representation parts and quality control. It
therefore requires complete knowledge of the system to be
developed as well as of the methods employed in the
development. The role of integration and quality management
in a large project may be seen to be partially equivalent to
that of a "chief programmer" in a chief programmer team.
There are four primary facets to this role:

1 Enforcement of Methods and Standards

On this technical management level, the use of
methods and standards and their corresponding
tools should be defined. Statistics gathering and
quality control data should assist in evaluating
the effectiveness of methods and tools. If
necessary, the latter have to be modified. It
should be possible to guarantee the use of
specific methods and tools (in specific versions)
by the development teams.

2 Integration

There should be means for imposing subsystem
interfaces; once defined these interfaces should
be physically controlled by the integration
management team as they design the integration
test plans according to these interfaces. Results
of work packages are internally delivered to the
integration managers who perform integration
testing, i.e. coordinate the simultaneous testing
of (all) the corresponding software subsystems.

3 Quality Control

Since integration management is concerned with
internal acceptance of peoples work during a
specific phase it should impose quality controls
before accepting an internal delivery. After
integration testing is performed, the consistency

and overall quality of the system representation considered should be checked.

4   Change Management

Because of its central technical role, integration and quality management should be the recipient of trouble reports and change requests. It should manage the processing of these requests, if necessary in collaboration with the project management level.

2.5.2   Configuration Control

Configuration control has to be applied to all the objects of information, held in an APSE database, which are generated, modified and used during the developoment and maintenance of a system.

The specific requirements for configuration control arise from the main characteristics of the demanding project, viz:

1   Development and maintenance are structured by life cycle activities which iteratively produce a multitude of objects representing the system at various levels of abstraction.

2   Development and maintenance are performed and managed by several teams of people who have various rights to access objects and who communicate and share objects in various ways.

3   The system exists in several versions at several sites during its lifetime.

Characteristics 1 and 3 necessitate a precise identification of objects and their components as well as a guaranteed coherence of versions. Characteristic 2 requires flexible access control and visibillity management. Finally characteristic 3 calls for the possibility of archiving and regenerating system versions. We consider these topics in more detail below.

1 Object Identification

The Configuration Control System (CCS) must be able to store objects which are parts of the representations of each stage of the Overall Method, record dependencies between these objects, and provide a naming scheme for accessing these objects.

It must be possible to represent the fact that some of the objects are composed of other objects. In general we will have a hierarchic structure in which objects at one level may be part of more than one object at a higher level. In other words the dependencies will form a network, not a tree.

2 Version Control

It must be possible to distinguish different versions of these objects, and to indicate whether they are to be treated as controlled or uncontrolled (see below).

The CCS must enforce a policy for deciding when a new version of an object should be generated, and when it should be marked controlled. It must implement a mechanism for maintaining consistency of the inter-object dependencies even when the objects exist in many versions.

3 Access Control and Visibility Management

The concept of controlled objects is important at all stages of the Life Cycle, but is most readily explained by an example from the Executable System Stage. We will not want to allow anyone to change a released version of a system, hence it must be marked as controlled, and preserved unchanged by the CCS. However it is essential to be able to modify development versions of a system, and these would be marked as uncontrolled. Implicitly any objects which form part of a controlled object must themselves be marked as controlled, or treated as if they were by the CCS. Obviously it must be possible to produce a new (controlled) version of the system and it may have objects in common with the previous controlled version.

The CCS must implement an integrity policy which controls access to, and the ability to change or delete, the database objects. The primary constraint on deletion is that it should not be possible to delete controlled objects, or objects which are used by controlled objects.

The CCS must be able to provide its facilities for a number of systems simultaneously, and for a number of teams working on different aspects of the same system at the same time. It must provide interfaces to the project management system and allow measurements to be made on the development and maintenance processes. It must also provide interfaces to the APSE tools to allow them to expoit the CCS facilities (and must prevent them from circumventing this interface).

4   Archiving and Regeneration

A further essential facility of a CCS is that it must be able to record the history of how and by whom, a particular object was created, in order that we may maintain management control over the development, or enhancement of the system. Additionally the CCS should allow us to be able to access or recreate historic versions of the system as we may wish to re-release old software. In many environments this means that configuration control must extend to archives as it will not be possible to maintain all the historic information on-line.

We believe these to be the most fundamental aspects of the requirements for the CCS, but recognise that it is very difficult to give a definitive requirement for configuration control. This is an area in which a considerable amount of additional research is required.

3

Outline of a coherent APSE

3.1 Development Methods

3.1.1 Introduction

We describe here the methods which we have investigated during the course of the study, and which, with one exception, we recommend as a starting point for the production of a coherent APSE. We describe the method for each level in the life cycle then discuss how well it satisfies the requirements laid down for it in section 2.4, and how it rates against the assessment criteria specified in section 2.2.5. We also consider alternative methods and potentially valuable extensions and enhancements to our chosen methods. In section 3.3 we discuss the coherency of the methods in the light of the criteria given in section 2.2.5, and we also consider ease of change for the method set as a whole.

The descriptions of each method are fairly brief. These descriptions are intended to give the reader some idea of the characteristics of the method, rather than to allow him to apply the method. Further information on the methods can be obtained from a number of sources. Quite detailed descriptions of the individual methods can be found in working papers from the study [Systems Designers Limited (1982a-h)], along with an example of the use of the methods. Annex 1 contains extracts from these working papers as an illustration of the notation and style of the methods. Finally further information on the methods can be found from the references cited in this chapter.

We base our judgement of the methods on the experiments we have performed during the study, documented

in [Systems Designers Limited (1982a-h)], and on the
published literature where it is relevant. In general the
methods satisfy the requirements so, for the sake of
brevity, we only describe the shortcomings of the methods
with respect to their requirements.

We do not give an exhaustive list of alternative
methods, nor do we make detailed comparative studies of the
alternatives. We do however note alternative methods and
tools of which we are aware which might either be directly
relevant for the level of representation under
consideration, or which are examples of good current
practice for the method under consideration. Thus our lists
of alternative methods might serve both as a starting point
for a comparative study of methods relevant to our chosen
interpretation of the life cycle model, and as an indication
of the type of tools which can be produced with "existing
technology".

Since some of the Development Methods are used
for more than one Level of Representation we only list the
differences between the first and subsequent uses of any
given method, again for the sake of brevity.

3.1.2 Requirements Expression - CORE
3.1.2.1 Method

CORE [Systems Designers Limited (1978), Systems
Designers Limited (1982a), Goldsack and Downes (1982)] is
addressed specifically at the problems of establishing a
Requirements Expression. The CORE method is expected to be
used by an Analyst who is trying to establish the RE by
eliciting information from a set of User Representatives.
There is also a Customer Authority who is responsible for
resolving discrepancies between the different User
Representatives viewpoints and for finally accepting the RE.

CORE provides guidelines for establishing the
relationships between the viewpoints of the system held by
the User Representatives, known as a Viewpoint Hierarchy.
The CORE method consists of establishing the Viewpoint
Hierarchy, then interviewing the User Representatives (or

reading documents which describe their view of the system).
The User Representatives are interviewed in an order, based
on the Viewpoint Hierarchy, which enables the information
which they give readily to be checked for consistency with
the other views. A set of analyses are performed to ensure
that the views are consistent, and that they are
analytically complete.

CORE includes a phase for reliability assessment
which is an important aspect of any requirements analysis. A
further important aspect of the CORE analyses is that they
make it clear when the Requirement Expression has been
completed and the analysis should stop. This is something
which is not always easy to determine when an ad hoc
approach to the expression of requirements is adopted.

The CORE notation consists of diagrams,
supported by prose. There are diagrams showing data
relationships, and a further set of diagrams which show
functions, the functional dependencies, and the data flow
between the functions. The notation is hierarchic in
character and deliberately allows some ambiguity of
expression, particularly concerning the characteristics of
the data flows between functions. The notation also shows
temporal relationships between the functions and controls on
the functions governing the choice of alternatives and the
termination of iteration.

The analyses mentioned above validate the
internal consistency and logical completeness of the CORE
representation. The transformation is verified by checking
and acceptance of the RE by the Customer Authority as
described in section 2.4.3.

3.1.2.2 Satisfaction of Requirements

CORE very closely meets our requirements as set
out in Section 2.4, and is particularly strong in dealing
with the practicalities of eliciting requirements from a
group of people who hold only partial system views.

CORE is based on a well-defined, semi-formal,
notation. Whilst we believe formality of notation to be

generally desirable we do not believe that a fully formal method is appropriate to Requirements Expression. Thus we believe that CORE represents a satisfactory compromise between formality and practicality, given the nature of the problem it is addressing.

The CORE verification processes are not formal. It is possible to produce and check a CORE representation incrementally, hence it is comparatively easy to handle changes to a CORE representation. CORE is amenable to tool support. It would be fairly straightforward to develop a database for storing (textual) representations of CORE diagrams, together with a set of tools for performing CORE analyses.

Neither the notation nor the method preclude the reuse of existing standard components, but it seems extremely unlikely that reuse would occur in practice given the nature of the Requirement Expression process. This argument also applies to the System Specification.

CORE appears to be fairly easy to learn, from the point of view of understanding the diagrammatic notation, but we do not have any evidence from this experiment of the difficulty or otherwise of learning how to apply the method.

It is reasonably easy to accommodate changes within an RE based on CORE as the Viewpoint Hierarchy shows where we need to look for effects of the changes.

On a more philosophical note, the example system used in the experiment was one that had previously been built by one of the contributors, without use of any particular method. In the experiment a number of timing and synchronisation problems were found when performing the requirements analysis which had only appeared during testing when the system had been built previously. This experience lends credence to the hypothesis that the use of effective methods early in the life cycle simplifies the eventual implementation and maintenance.

3.1.2.3 Alternatives

There are a number of other notations aimed at Requirements Expression, e.g. PSL/PSA [Teichrow and Hershey (1977)] and SADT [Ross (1977)]. PSL/PSA is a good example of a notation and toolset for requirements expression and analysis. PSL/PSA also is applicable to the various design stages, and in fact may be better suited to design.

SADT is the nearest equivalent to CORE of which we are aware, indeed some of the CORE notation is derived from that used in SADT. As far as we can tell from the literature CORE is superior to SADT in three ways:

1 CORE deals with the systems environment, SADT does not;

2 CORE has a richer notation than SADT;

3 it is possible to perform more powerful analyses on CORE representations than it is on SADT representations.

CORE and SADT seem to be the only two major candidates for a Requirements Expression method which satisfy our requirements.

3.1.2.4 Extensions and Enhancements

CORE commendably deals with reliability issues. However it would be useful if it separately addressed issues of integrity, particularly in the areas of validation of input to the system. Some notational extensions to CORE would also be desirable, for example, to deal with complex interlinked data structures.

3.1.3 System Specification - The A-7 Techniques
3.1.3.1 Method

The method which we advocate for System Specification is a modified form of the techniques developed

by Parnas and his colleagues the re-implementation of the
A-7 aircraft software [Heninger et al (1978)]. We made the
modifications to the method whilst developing the System
Specification in our experiment, and the reasons for making
the changes are documented in [Systems Designers Limited
(1982b)].

The notation is concerned with data items,
functions, and the events which cause the functions to be
applied to the data items. The notation is essentially flat,
i.e. it only allows for one level of functions, rather than
a hierarchy of functions. The data items are described in
three distinct classes:

RWAI - Real World Available Information: data items
which are avilable in the systems environment;

LODI - Logical Output Data Items: Data items output by
the system to the environment;

ADI - Auxiliary Data Items: data items retained by the
system.

These data items are all described in a
syntactic notation which defines their logical form, and
which may be used to specify the values which the data items
can take.

The functions are classed as being either
"demand" or "periodic" with the obvious interpretation. The
transfer characteristics of the functions are defined either
by tables similar to truth tables, or by pseudo-code. These
forms are equivalent and relate the values of the outputs
from the function to the values of the function inputs.

The mapping between the inputs and the outputs
and the peripheral devices attached to the (hardware) system
are stated in the System Specification. Finally some
auxiliary information which may be useful in the
implementation is recorded. For example information on
expected changes may help the guidance of the design on

information hiding principles.

The guidelines for developing this specification are as outlined in section 2.4.

3.1.3.2 Satisfaction of Requirements

We believe that our modified form of the A-7 techniques meet the requirements for System Specification. They provide a clear specification, which contains a very large part, if not all, of the information necessary to allow the system to be designed and built. The "event-based" nature of the notation makes the A-7 techniques much better suited to specifying embedded systems than, for example, information systems.

The representation combines formal notation with prose. The verification within the SS representation is formal, being primarily concerned with showing the completeness and correctness of the tables. It is possible to perform the analyses progressively on a function by function basis, although some overall consistency checks are required. The check on the transformation is informal due to the nature of the RE.

The techniques would be amenable to tool support, in particular for checking the consistency and completeness of the tables defining the transfer characteristics of the functions.

The A-7 Techniques give a systematic method for developing a System Specification which is structured in such a way that the different parts of the specification are highly orthogonal. This means that (the inevitable) changes in specification can be accommodated with comparative ease. For example the change of a physical output device would impact the part of the specification dealing with the logical to physical mapping, but would not affect either the definition of the LODI, or of the functions which generated the outputs.

Further the "Pragmatic Formality" of the techniques, i.e. the careful blend of formal and informal notations, makes them easy to learn and apply, but nonetheless yields highly precise specifications.

We believe that the use of the A-7 techniques will result in the production of very high quality System Specifications, which will be suitable for use as the primary reference document for system design and development.

3.1.3.3 Alternatives

There are quite a large number of methods relevant to the System Specification and Abstract Functional Specification levels of representation. Many of these methods are described by terms like "software requirements specification" but most are really high level design languages (in our terminology) as even the highest level representation are concerned with functional breakdowns, processes etc., e.g. [Zave (1982)].

HDM [Robinson et al (1976)] addresses software design as a series of "abstract machines". The higher levels of machine are appropriate at the SS and AFS levels. Similarly the more abstract representations in HOS [Hamilton and Zeldin (1976)] are relevant to these levels of representaion. SREM [Alford (1977)] is a good example of a high level design notation and toolset which is frequently described as being aimed at "software requirements".

3.1.3.4 Extensions and Enhancements

We have already made considerable extensions and enhancements to the A-7 techniques, and there are no further modifications which we would suggest at present for their application to System Specification. We do expect however that further modifications may be found necessary to ensure general applicability of the method.

3.1.4 Abstract Functional Specification - A-7 Techniques

3.1.4.1 Method

The AFS [Systems Designers Limited (1982c)] is produced using the A-7 notation, further extended to be able to represent the hierarchical composition of functions. The production of the AFS is governed by the design guidelines mentioned in section 2.4, but is still heavily dependent on the skill of the designer.

The mapping between the AFS and SS is not necessarily straightforward. For example in our experiment there were a number of functions in the AFS which contributed to the implementation of more than one function in the SS. This organisation was chosen for reasons of efficiency. Our implementation contained less than ten tasks but if we had implemented the system directly in the user-oriented form suggested by the SS then there would have been several thousand tasks in the system, and the system would have utterly failed to meet its performance requirements.

3.1.4.2 Satisfaction of Requirements

These techniques were not as satisfactory for the AFS as for the SS because the notation for representing the composition of functions is inadequate. In essence the problem is in combining the control flow concepts necessary to define the functional composition with the notation for describing the transfer characteristics of the individual functions in such a way that we can deduce the transfer characteristics of the composite functions.

3.1.4.3 Alternatives

The alternative methods which we mentioned under the SS are also relevant here - perhaps more so than at the SS. From our limited study of the alternative methods they seem to assume a simpler mapping between levels than we believe to be necessary between SS and AFS. Specifically many of the methods assume that the structure of the requirement and the structure of the design for the system are isomorphic. In our example this constraint would have meant that the implemented system would have completely failed to meet it's performance targets. This strengthens our belief that the alternative methods are really concerned with high level design, not system specification.

At the AFS level it may be appropriate to perform simulations or rapid prototyping of the system under development. DREAM [Riddle (1981)] is an example of a methodology and toolset which tries to give an early appreciation of the behaviour of the system being developed by means of simulation.

3.1.4.4 Extensions and Enhancements

An essential enhancement to the A-7 techniques is the improvement of the notation for showing function composition. Some additional notation for specifying, or estimating, performance and program size parameters would be advantageous.

3.1.5 Module Specification – Ada and ANNA
3.1.5.1 Method

In our experiment we were concerned entirely with specifying the behaviour of the software. In a practical methodology we would also require notations for describing the hardware structures, and the hardware to software mappings, as is done, for example, in PERSPECTIVE [Systems Designers Limited (1983)].

ANNA [Krieg-Bruckner and Luckham (1980)] was used in conjunction with Ada [Department of Defense (1980a)] in the production of the Module Specification [Systems Designers Limited (1982d)] in our experiment. We presume that it is unnecessary to describe Ada, but we present a brief description of ANNA.

ANNA is a notation for annotating Ada programs with packages. It is based on the predicate calculus, but includes extensions to deal with concepts, such as array update, which are foreign to the predicate calculus. An ANNA specification for a package consists of a collection of boolean expressions all evaluating to TRUE. These expressions state invariants for data objects and for the subprograms visible in the package. It is possible to introduce auxiliary variables (e.g. to represent data hidden within a module), in order to simplify the expression of the invariants.

Since the experiment with ANNA was completed a second version of ANNA [Krieg-Bruckner et al (1982)] has been produced. The comments below apply to the 1980 version of ANNA and are not necessarily valid comments on the 1982 version of the language.

The contents of the modules and their usage relationships are outlined in a Module Decomposition document [Systems Designers Limited (1982e)]. The Module Decomposition is synopsis of the MS, provided to give the system implementors a clear overview of the software structure.

3.1.5.2 Satisfaction of Requirements

Ada was entirely satisfactory for its role in Module Specification.

ANNA does allow one to perform the basic task of Module Specification, that of specifying the semantics of the subprograms within each module, with reasonable accuracy. ANNA is not entirely satisfactory for Module Specification as it stands because of it's inability to deal with tasks. Formal treatment of concurrency seems to be currently beyond the "state of the art" in program specification, except for fairly constrained situations, so this is a general problem and is not just a criticism of ANNA.

However, even if this shortcoming were resolved, we are dubious about the applicability of ANNA because of the difficulty we found in using the language. The difficulty came primarily because of the low level of abstraction (high level of detail) at which we ended up working. This difficulty may have been partly due to the nature of our problem, and our inexperience in using ANNA, but we believe that it was due in large measure to the properties of ANNA itself. The biggest deficiency is the lack of a mechanism for handling abstraction without explicitly introducing it by auxiliary Ada text. More minor problems with ANNA are discussed in [Systems Designers

Limited (1982d)].

In summary we do not believe that the benefits of using ANNA are sufficiently great to justify its use except under exceptional circumstances, e.g. where we wish to formally verify the properties of part of a program. However we do believe that ANNA would be much more effective if we did wish to perform verification, as it seems to come into its own for annotating implementations, rather than specifying what an implementation should do.

Thus, whilst we commend the formality of ANNA, we cannot recommend it for general use for Module Specification. We believe however that given suitable extensions to ANNA and adequate tool support that ANNA may become practical for specification purposes in a wide spectrum of applications.

Both formal and progressive verification of ANNA annotations are possible.

Tool support is quite feasible for ANNA both for passive checking of the representation, and for active prompting for information (see section 3.4.2). In principle standard Ada and ANNA components could be used in this, and subsequent representations, and we can see no reason why this should not be possible and beneficial in practice.

The concepts of ANNA were quite simple to learn, although difficult to learn how to apply. The details of the language are rather complex due to the intricacies of Ada which it is designed to annotate.

ANNA statements are quite hard to modify especially if they are of significant size or complexity. This would be much less of a problem if a support tool which checked for consistency and completeness of statements were available.

3.1.5.3 Alternatives

The HDM methodology [Robinson et al (1976)] incorporates a specification language, SPECIAL, which is capable of being used in a manner quite similar to that intended for ANNA. SPECIAL is not directly applicable to Ada however a new version of SPECIAL, known as SPECIAL-A [Roubine (1982)], which is directly aimed at specifying the properties of Ada programs, has now been defined. SPECIAL-A does not deal with tasks, but has features which directly address most of the other criticisms which we had of ANNA. Perhaps most significantly it has a notation for dealing with hierarchies of abstract machines, and for specifying the mappings between the levels in the hierarchy. SPECIAL-A seems to be worthy of further consideration for this role in the Life Cycle.

ANNA does not deal with concurrency. Two notations which have been developed for dealing with concurrency are CCS [Milner (1980)] and Temporal Logic [Schwarz and Melliar-Smith (1981)]. It would be valuable to study the application of these two techniques to the specification of Ada tasking. It is also possible to take a direct axiomatic approach to the specification and verification of the properties of Ada tasks as demonstrated in [Barringer and Mearns (1982)]. This approach is interesting although it may be hard to apply in practice because of the complexity of the axioms.

3.1.5.4 Extensions and Enhancements

ANNA does not cater for Ada programs with tasks. Although we managed to circumvent this problem in our experiment our solution was not entirely satisfactory, and a better solution must be found if ANNA is to be applicable to programs with tasks. This could be done either by extending ANNA or by using an additional notation such as CCS.

Individual statements in ANNA can be very complex. ANNA does not currently have facilities, such as macros, to allow complex statements to be factored in order to increase their intelligibility. The lack of facilities in ANNA for abstraction also tends to increase the complexity of the ANNA statements. The lack of the concept of intermediate states in ANNA makes certain types of subprogram very difficult to annotate correctly. These problems must be resolved if ANNA is to have wide applicability.

We remind the reader that these comments are aimed at the 1980 version of ANNA and that significant enhancements have been made to the language since then, as documented in [Krieg-Bruckner et al (1982)].

3.1.6 Module Design - Ada and ANNA
3.1.6.1 Method

We proposed Ada and ANNA for this Level of Representation in the model. In our experiment we found that sufficient information was present in the Module Specification to allow the Module Code to be produced directly, without going through Module Design. This being the case our conclusions regarding satisfaction of requirements are based on conjecture, rather than experimental evidence. We make no conclusions on Alternatives or Extensions and Enhancements.

3.1.6.2 Satisfaction of Requirements

We expect that Ada and ANNA would be roughly as satisfactory in this role as for the Module Specification. It is possible however that some of the problems in using ANNA would be less severe than in the Module Specification as we are dealing with a less abstract representation of the final module code.

3.1.7 Module Code - Ada and ANNA
3.1.7.1 Method

We used Ada and ANNA to produce the Module Code. We did not generate a new ANNA annotation for the Module Code as we believed that the relevant parts of the Module Specification contained a clear specification of the Code. Consequently we will not make any further assessment of the suitability or otherwise of ANNA.

3.1.7.2 Satisfaction of Requirements

Ada proved quite adequate for this task. However the syntax of Ada was found to be complex, containing many special cases, which made it very difficult to learn and to remember. The Ada Language Reference Manual (LRM) [Department of Defense (1980a)] is written in a style which tends to exacerbate this problem. The new manual [Department of Defense (1982a)] seems no better in this respect. There is a clear need for a good teaching text for Ada.

The separation of Package Specification and Implementation helped considerably in producing separate Module Specification and Module Code representations. This is an aspect of Ada which we can thoroughly commend.

Despite our reservations about the detailed design of the language, Ada represents a significant step forward from languages in common use for producing embedded systems.

3.1.8   Executable System

We did not produce executable code so we can add no comments about this stage in the life cycle.

3.1.9   Summary

We are confident that CORE and the A-7 techniques are satisfactory for performing the tasks of Requirements Expression and System Specification. We believe that the A-7 techniques can be extended to provide a satisfactory basis for the Abstract Functional Specification.

ANNA is much less satisfactory and we would recommend that SPECIAL-A be studied to assess its capabilities for the Module Specification role. Even if SPECIAL-A does prove to be a significant improvement on ANNA we will still not have an adequate formalism for dealing with concurrency. We can only suggest that other techniques, e.g. Temporal Logic, CCS, be considered for use as an adjunct to the Ada oriented specification languages.

3.2   Management Methods

3.2.1   Configuration Control

3.2.1.1   Introduction

Configuration control has only recently received attention in connection with programming environments. Methods are evolving but, as yet, no method appears to be sufficiently powerful, or sufficiently widely accepted to impose itself as a candidate with which this study could have experimented.

Thus in performing the study we have had to provide a partially original framework as well as building on existing work. Hopefully this will provide a constructive starting point for further work in this area. We start by describing the system which we have taken as our starting point in studying configuration control.

3.2.1.2   The Chosen Method - SDL2020

3.2.1.2.1   Background

Our chosen method has succesfully been used on demanding industrial projects in the domain of embedded real-time systems. The system was originally developed under the name SGDL [Maissonneuve et al (1981), Maissonneuve (1981) and Caillet et al (1982)] by CIT-Alcatel, in conjunction with TECSI-Software, who now market the system as a product under the name SDL2020. This system has been in use on a day-to-day basis for nearly two years for configuration control in the development and maintenance of the telephone switching system E10-S and its dozen different applications.

The underlying model of SDL2020 seems to provide a good starting point for consideration of an APSE configuration control system. Specifically, it offers the necessary functionality and takes the uniform view of the production and manipulation of data items which is necessary for dealing with a variety of methods. Moreover, the model provides a basis for the formulation of project management methods.

We have therfore based our configuration control

work on the SDL2020 model. We describe the basic concepts of
the model below, and Annex 2 describes the data model in
detail, augmented with the entities and relationships
provided for project management.

3.2.1.2.2   The Product Concept

SDL2020 is based on the principle that all the
data objects which have to be put under configuration
control can be administered and controlled by a single
method, _independent_ of their type. All these objects are
called "products" reflecting the fact that they will be
produced as the result of some activity in the APSE.

The successive system representations of the
life cycle can, for instance, be seen as products. The
corresponding transformations are then simply product
generation activities. From this point of view the life
cycle model corresponds to a network of "assembly lines".
Each position on the assembly line may be seen as being
represented by a product. In this sense a product
incorporates also the notion of a step in an overall
production process and the corresponding "human" function in
an organisation.

The term "product" is used in the sense of "a
result of a stage of the fabrication process" rather than in
the usual sense of a finished commercially available
product. Thus a product can itself be used in the production
of another, more complex, product. In order to maintain a
complete history SDL2020 therefore records both how a
product was produced and where it has been used. Examples of
products are module design documents, module sources,
objects, binaries, executable systems or subsystems.

It is important to recognise that any
configuration control method needs to identify the "grains"
whose evolution has to be controlled. These grains may be of
different sizes. They could be small data items
representing, say, details of a system specification, or
they could be the total system specification document
itself. The method presented here leaves, in principle, the

choice of the grain size of products up to the user. However we take the standpoint that a complete system has to be a product so that version control can at least reflect the completion of new versions of a system.

In summary, the representations produced in performing a project are, independent of their specific type, subjected to configuration control as "products". Data objects which are part of these products are administered as parts and not as products in their own right.

Since products are undergoing constant evolution there generally exist several instances of a product at any given time. This would at least suggest that a product must be seen as an ordered set of "versions", rather than as a single product. However, this simple differentiation does not adequately reflect the reality of many production contexts where there is a need to distinguish different levels or qualities of versions.

For this reason the model discussed here views a product as a tree with at most four levels. The leaves of the tree represent specific instances of a product whilst the root and the intermediate nodes represent sets of instances. The model contains four levels because of the different ways in which new instances of a product may be brought into existence.

The highest intermediate level (i.e. that immediately below the root) is known as the "version" level. It reflects functional changes from one product version to another.

The next intermediate level is known as the "edition" level. It reflects changes in the composition of a version of a product, in terms of the components or tools used, from one edition to another.

The level of the leaves is known as the "iteration" level. It reflects simple revisions of an edition of a version of a product from one iteration to another.

Consequently an instance of a product can be identified by a path in the product tree from the root to a leaf. Thus each product instance is identified by a name and three parameters: a version number, an edition number, and an iteration number.

The product concept which is at the heart of this model is described in more detail in Annex 2 which contains an outline of a general data model for the APSE.

3.2.1.2.3 Use of Production Tools can be standarised

A product is created under SDL2020 by means of standard procedures. This fabrication procedure contains all of the details related to the production of a product along with the associated calls to the development tools in use. The procedure is stored by SDL2020 as an integral part of the product. The system allows fabrication procedures to be defined and catalogued, and then imposes the use of these standardised catalogued procedures, hence limiting the proliferation of "personal kits" of software tools.

This approach does not however limit the choice of tools. The underlying concept of products with versions, editions and iterations is quite general, and various classes of tool can be related to this concept. Thus the system can accommodate management, project control and documentation tools, as well as those which support actual software development.

3.2.1.2.4 Production History is conserved and exploited

The production history of a product shows both the other products that were used in its fabrication and all of the tools that were employed in the process. The product is stored together with its production history in the APSE database.

It is therefore possible to search for either the component parts of a product, or the products of which a specific product is a part. This capability allows any product to be regenerated from its history. The regenerated product may be anything from a single module to a complete system.

In this way, SDL2020 provides automatic support

for updates, versions and releases. The fact that regeneration is automatic also ensures that it is performed consistently.

3.2.1.2.5 Access is controlled by hierarchical libraries

All products under the control of SDL2020 are grouped into libraries. One library could correspond, for example, to the set of products developed by one team, and could be used for all storage and manipulation of the team's private files.

Shared files can be stored in one or several reference libraries which are arranged hierarchically and which may be searched in hierarchical order. Unless otherwise specified, the procedures for generating or regenerating a product search the current library by default for its component parts, and then if necessary an ordered list of libraries. In this way, by controlling the contents of reference libraries, it is possible to ensure that only "approved" versions of certain products are used by production teams.

3.2.1.3 Satisfaction of Requirements

The elaborate product structure of the model satisfies several requirements. It provides a naming scheme and it allows the recording of dependencies among products in the form of a network. It allows different "versions" of products to be distinguished and even caters for a gradation of "versions" with different qualities. Functional variants correspond to the versions of the model; variants of the same functionality but for different purposes (expressed in different languages, for debugging or for delivery etc.) correspond to the editions; and successor variants or, simply, revisions correspond to the iterations.

Due to the different product levels it is possible to decide explicitly when a new version or edition of a product should be generated whilst the generation of new iterations is automatic.

In order that the consistency of the

inter-product dependencies can be verified all the
components of a product must be uniquely identified by a
combination of their name, version, edition and iteration.
Name uniqueness is guaranteed by the concept of the product
base in which product names are generated. The uniqueness of
the version, iteration and edition numbers is guaranteed by
the automation of the product generation and regeneration
procedures.

The requirement for a distinction between
controlled and uncontrolled versions is satisfied by the
library concept. Teams have different access rights with
respect to libraries. The library managed by a team contains
uncontrolled versions whereas reference libraries which are
only accessible for reading by a team may contain controlled
versions. There may exist different library levels of
uncontrolled and controlled versions for which the search
rules can be specified with respect to each team (concept of
the hierarchical search). Both controlled and uncontrolled
versions can be shared.

The use of specific interfaces to APSE-tools can
be enforced through the generation procedures which may also
provide the hooks for management and measurement procedures.

The complete history of all the products is
kept, so that "Historic" versions of products can be
regenerated. The provision of these regeneration facilities,
and the inclusion of integration mechanisms in the methods,
reflects the fact that the model has been conceived for the
demanding project where several system versions are worked
upon simultaneously by several teams.

The model represents a programming support
environment which never forgets, but it does allow
controlled deletion of products. The control imposed is that
no product may be deleted whilst it is referred to as a
component of some other product.

Although the model satisfies all the
configuration control requirements in one form or another it
must be pointed out that it does so only for data objects
which are of sufficient grain size to be treated as

products. Complete configuration control of small sized data
items identified by a microscopic view of a product
representation (cf 2.2) still remains a problem.

The evolution of microscopic data items with
respect to the enclosing product can be controlled if the
enclosing product is regarded as being changed whenever one
of its microscopic data items has been changed. However, if
it is desired to show the evolution of microscopic items
independently of their enclosing product then the model is
not satisfactory in this respect.

3.2.1.4 Alternative methods

To our knowledge none of the configuration
control systems which are in use or under construction
satisfy the above requirements as well as the system
outlined above. Consequently instead of discussing these
other systems - which are not really alternative methods -
in detail, we will briefly describe the similarities and
shortcomings of these systems.

Only the CADES system [McGuffin et al (1979)]
deals with the microscopic view of representations. For the
control and maintenance of the relationships between data
items it uses sophisticated data base mechanisms. Most of
the other systems consider a "module", which corresponds to
our "product", as the unit of configuration control e.g.
[Cheatham et al (1981), Wasserman et al (1981), Schmidt
(1982), Tichy (1980)]. The general "product" view appears in
[Cooprider (1978)] and as a "typed product" view in [Tichy
(1980)].

In most systems there is just one numbering
level for products [e.g. Cheatham (1981), Wasserman et al
(1981)]. When a product is changed its version number is
automatically incremented.

There seem to be two different approaches to
capturing a complete system description. In our model and
others e.g. [Intermetrics (1981), Cheatham et al (1981)] a
system is viewed as a network of products each with their
associated generation history. The other approaches describe

a system by a monolithic system description in a text file [Notkin and Habermann (1981), Schmidt (1982)].

The requirements for demanding projects are nearly always ignored. Even in CADES the integration of subsystems which have been under independent development is not completely controlled by the system. At least CADES has its "region" structure which allows one to specify access rights for ordinary users. Regions correspond to our libraries but in CADES the concept of a product base as the controlled name space of products is missing. In [Cheatham et al (1981) and Wasserman et al(1981)] integration mechanisms and controlled sharing of products are not treated. There seems to be no relation maintained between the descriptions of different system states in [Schmidt (1982)].

Several systems are specialised to the control of source modules [Rochkind (1975), Cargill (1980), Schmidt (1982)]. As an extreme example [Schmidt (1982)] is tailored specifically to the language MESA. (Note that the SCCS-system of [Rochkind (1975)] is contained in the SDL2020-system).

The model presented here fits the Ada Integrated Environment of [Intermetrics (1981)] very well. Its "system attributes". "category", "access" and "history" correspond to our product types together with the generation procedures, our command and library access rights, and our "history", respectively.

The user-defined relationships between APSE-products required in the form of "group maps" and "associated attributes" in [Stenning et al (1981)] correspond to our "sys"-products (see section 3.2.2.2.4) and type-dependent relationships, respectively.

The Harvard-PDS [Cheatham et al (1981)] is planned to support "fine grained version control with all tools providing incremental rederivation of derived modules after changes in their parent modules". But still the module is the subject of version numbering. The version number associated with an entity contained in a module is that of the module at the time of the entity's creation or modification.

The notions of a module being "up-to-date" or "safely deletable" are the same as in our model.

3.2.1.5 Extensions and Enhancements

Configuration control is a highly complex subject although a project of the scale of our experiment does not show up the true complexities of the subject. A particular problem which we have pointed out several times is the maintenance of the consistency of relationships between atomic data items as well as between the documents of which the atomic items are parts. A solution to this problem would be a very valuable enhancement to a configuration control system.

Our model offers a coarse grain solution to this problem where a "product" (which is itself a database entity) represents a group of entities and relationships, see Figure 3.1. The consistency of the relationships between products is maintained. Interproduct references however still pose a problem for consistency control. Should a local change of data item "a" within product P1 lead to a new product iteration? Does it lead to copying of all the data items of P1 and the resetting of pointers from data items of product P2, for instance, to the new copy of "a".

This is still a research problem. Different solutions may have to be found depending on storage and performance considerations. Probably research into specific data base mechanisms is necessary. Within CADES, for instance, the desire to obtain a reasonable fine grain solution led to important modifications of the basic data base management system, however with the effect of poor performance.

According to the purpose of the study to show the feasibility of an APSE development in the near future, we take the standpoint that the coarse grain solution proposed is satisfactory but that interproduct references between atomic data items should be established by analysis

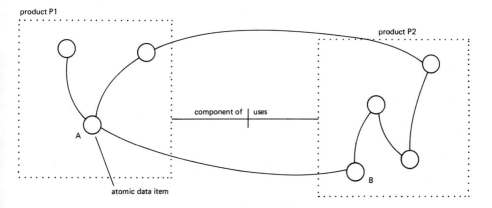

Figure 3.1   Inter-product relationships

tools. Further these atomic data items should be stored so that they allow detailed "browsing" through the documents and should act as the data for certain analyses. The atomic data items should not be used at present for change propagation purposes. Change propagation should be performed on the "macroscopic" product level.

There is another problem involved with changes for which the study has not worked out a detailed solution.

Control over the handling of changes will be extremely difficult because of the range of possibilities for reprocessing after a change. One possibility is that a module in a program is changed in such a way that there are no consequent changes which have to be made to the source code of other modules, so it would be desirable to provide automatic recompilation of the dependent modules. A different possibility is that some of the dependent modules will need to be changed and/or there are other related changes which have to be made. In this case automatic recompilation of dependent modules would be counter-productive.

The picture becomes more complex when we realise that there are quite a large number of reprocessing options, and that we also have to consider the relationships between the levels of representations, as well as within one level. Since the reprocessing which we will need to perform depends on the semantics of the change it is unlikely that the APSE database, or the configuration control system, can decide which reprocessing option to apply. The best they can do is to provide a wide range of reprocessing options, and possibly allow the tools to invoke these options, since the tools may well have enough semantic information to decide which option is appropriate.

3.2.2 Project Management
3.2.2.1 Introduction

Management methods so far have very much depended on the "personal taste" within an organisation. On the one hand, it is quite easy to conceive what management is about and how it could be done, on the other hand it is in this area that very often the capital errors are committed which lead to project failures.

The literature about project management ranges from very valuable nearly "folkloristic" guidelines, based on specific experiences e.g. [Brooks (1975)], to comprehensive and voluminous methodologies such as SDM/70 [Atlantic Software (1970)]. There is considerable agreement in principle about the methods, for instance about the structuring of projects into phases. But since these methods are not related to specific life cycle activities or their methods and representations they give the impression of skeletons bare of the vital flesh.

The methods outlined here are not based on one candidate method. They have their roots in our own experience and in the general management culture expressed in the literature. However, we have tried to tie them intimately to the development methods and to the configuration control method in the spirit of a coherent APSE.

3.2.2.2 Description of the Chosen Method
3.2.2.2.1 Overview

This outline proceeds very much along the lines of the requirements for project management (cf 2.5.1). A detailed description of the underlying data model and of specific mechanisms is given in Annex 2.

The information required to carry out the management functions is either contained within the actual system documents or is very closely related to them. This is because the documents representing the system at any life cycle level are the tangible results of the production process which has to be managed, and they indicate which documents have to be produced by the next life cycle activity.

Hence, planning and organisation of a future phase have to be based on the sequence of life cycle levels - for instance the system specification has to be produced

after the requirements expression. Similarly the planning
and organisation are based on the contents of the current
system representation - for instance the module designs
which have to be produced depend on the modules which have
been identified in the module specification.

As a corollary, project control over the current
life cycle level has to monitor the production of certain
documents. In this case, progress data depend directly on
the status of these documents.

These relationships between management
functions, development activities and documents are captured
in the data model.

3.2.2.2.2 Project Planning and Organisation

In the data model, a project represents the
overall task of developing or modifying a system.

The detailed work programme is described by
specific tasks which are assigned to individuals. In order
to cater for organisations which have several management
levels, tasks may be decomposed into subtasks, and so on,
until the lowest level tasks are of such a size and
complexity that they can be accomplished by one person in a
reasonable amount of time. These lowest level tasks, at
least, each have to produce a tangible result in the form of
a document.

Before describing the methods, we give an
overview of the basic steps of planning and organisation in
tabular form. Each step is named, its objectives are listed,
and the resultant data structure is identified.

No.	Name	Objectives	Result
1	WORK BREAKDOWN	. Justification and description of tasks . Task Decomposition . Establishment of task dependencies	Work Breakdown Structure (WBS)
2	ESTIMATION	. Effort Estimation . Skill requirements analysis	Weighted WBS
3	PLANNING	. Man-power loading of tasks and planning . Resource requirements analysis	Plan
4	ORGANISATION	. Assignments to people . Resource assignments . Definition of management structure	Project Guide

Work Breakdown

The detailed work programme is described by a
task structure. The decomposition of tasks may only be
defined down to a certain management level. A subsequent
phase of the management activity may then refine the tasks
down to individual work assignments. The task structure will
closely reflect the life cycle levels and the system
structure.

These ideas are best illustrated by Figure 3.2
which sketches the work breakdown of the first phase of a
project. There are two levels of management in the first
phase. On the project management level, the task is the
development of a new system. With this task are associated
the tentative budget, delivery dates etc. According to the
life cycle model, this task can be decomposed into several
tasks of which the first to be performed may be the
specification. This task is further decomposed according to
the overall development method into two tasks. The first of
these two tasks has to produce the requirements expression
document (RE), the second one has to produce at least two
products, the system specification document (SS), and the

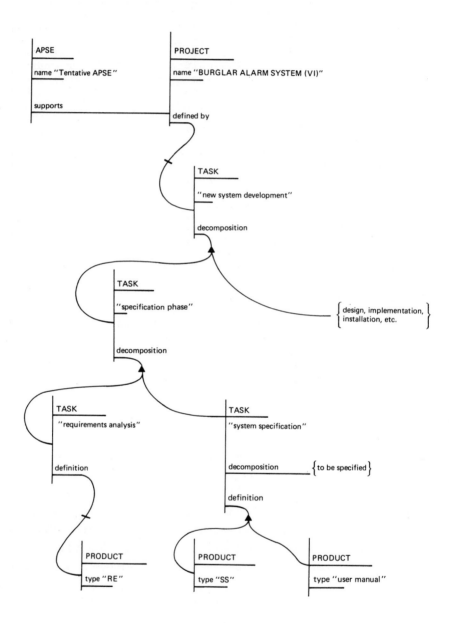

Figure 3.2   Work breakdown structure of first project phase

user's manual (or at least a part thereof).

The time dependencies between tasks are shown by the before/after relationships.

The second level tasks corresponding to the phases of design, implementation etc. may have been identified but not yet decomposed further since their decomposition depends on the results of the specification phase. The work breakdown of these future phases starts with these high level management tasks. Similarly, once the requirements expression has been developed sufficiently, the task of producing the system specification can be further decomposed on the basis of the contents of the RE document.

The work is thus broken down naturally and in harmony with the system structure and the evolution of the system representations.

Effort Estimation

The candidate method which we propose is a combination of two kinds of estimation techniques: a statistical and a semantic one.

Statistical methods have been described in [Walston and Felix (1977) and Boehm (1981)]. Based on large collections of data on project behaviour and on task lists, these methods permit the project manager to evaluate the influence of environmental factors such as know-how, administration, know-how transfer, and organisation on the productivity and quality of the development effort.

Semantic methods go back to the work of Halstead [Halstead (1977)]. They deal with the complexity of the development of a software system in a linguistic approach, based upon the following observations:

1   There is a very strong correlation between the types of activity in the software life-cycle, and the linguistic complexity of the end documents of these activities. One of the objectives of producing the microscopic view of these early specification documents is to reveal the actual

correlations.

2   There is an equally strong correlation between
    the volumes of the end documents for each of the
    successive activities in the life-cycle.

       One could express both correlations as: the same
basic semantic content is present in each of the levels of
design representation in the life cycle model, but it is
expanded in detail at each level of representation. Clearly
the level of semantic information present in the
Requirements Expression and System Specification is
different to that in any of the levels of design
representation.
       These observations make it possible to produce
an a priori estimate of design and development effort, very
early in a project life, based upon an early design
specification document, e.g. the AFS. Correction of this
estimate may then be seen as "follow up" or readjustment
based on a larger set of documents, as more and more
documents are produced.
       Experience, reported in [Keller (1979), Piquet
(1982)] shows that the Semantic Method is directly usable if
its application conditions are given, i.e. if the above
observations can be made with respect to the development
methods employed. But it has also been found that the
semantic method has to be combined with a statistical method
since environment factors can modify the effort estimation
by a factor of 3 to 4.
       It is not difficult to see how the results of
effort estimation can lead to the evaluation of the
effort-related attributes of the tasks, including the
management tasks.

Planning
       Once the work has been broken down and the
effort required has been estimated, the plan can be
generated in the planning step. This step evaluates the task

attributes of duration, earliest start and finish, and latest start and finish for a chosen man-power loading, taking into account the task dependencies.

Planning methods of this kind are well-known and form the basis of all PERT and critical-path management techniques. They may take deadlines or effort limits as their boundary conditions, and they should also lead to a quantitative assessment of the human and material resources needed according to the plan.

The necessary parameters for this analysis (e.g. computer time and equipment needed for a certain "type" of task) can initially be evaluated by estimation and, later on, they can be based on statistics.

Organisation

According to the plan, people and material resources have to be linked to tasks, and the management structure has to be defined. In a production context with unlimited resources and robot like human beings, the method would be straightforward. But in reality, this step is the most delicate one, requiring significant management skill. It is delicate, since it has to take into account not only facts like the limited availability of resources and the existence of certain teams in certain offices but it has to consider a large amount of non-quantifiable data and the probability of future events. Many of these data are of psychological and sociological nature, including likes and dislikes of individuals, and the problems of staff turnover.

Management has to fit people and organisational structure in the best possible way to the plan given this sort of unquantifiable constraint.

Although management has to consider data which are of a great variety (and which may even change their nature with cultural and economic changes within the Production Context) it should be possible for an approximate project guide to be generated.

At this stage, the "picture" of the project as resulting from the work breakdown has evolved so that:

1   Tasks   are assigned to persons   who   are   grouped
    into teams, lead by a person.

2   Most task attributes have been evaluated.

Note   that   the   management tasks are explicitly
represented   so   that   their   requirements   in   terms   of
organisation   and   communication   effort   has   also   been
evaluated.   Further,   where   the   available resources do not
match, the attributes and relationships remain open.

This   "picture" has to be analysed by management
who   have   to   vary   it   in   order   to   arrive   at   a closer
approximation   to   the   "best"   fit   under   the   given
circumstances.

The   method   for   these   iterations of the steps
leading to a project guide is discussed below.

Finally, in the organisation step, the rights of
teams   and   persons   to   access   database   entities, and the
Communication paths between persons have to be defined.

Access   rights   are   defined   through   the
configuration   control system. Every product is contained in
a Library which is managed by a team.   The members of a team
have complete control over the   products in their libraries.
For each library an ordered list   of   other libraries can be
associated which defines the visibility   of products outside
the   teams   own library.   For details   see   the   data   model
description in Annex 2.

Communication   paths   could   be derived from the
project   guide   which   shows   management levels, person/team
relationships,   and   task   dependencies.   Alternatively they
could   be   defined   explicitly by Management. Communication
paths   are   used   to   signal   events.   For   instance,   upon
completion   of   a   task   this   fact   can be signalled to the
person   responsible   for   a   dependent   task and to the team
leader.   Necessary   validation   and   review   tasks   can   be
prompted this way, e.g. when implementation of document A is
reported, the reviewers of this   document may find a note in

their electronic mailbox telling them to start the task of
reviewing document A. The "reviewer" could, of course, also
be a tool in the APSE. The processing of trouble reports and
maintenance requests can be programmed along the
communication paths.

The MONSTR system [Cashman and Holt (198Ø)] has
implemented this idea. It generates a protocol-driven
software trouble reporting system from a description of
communication pathways in the form of a state diagram.

The correct sequencing of a number of steps of a
complex operation can be described and prompted in the same
way. An example of such an operation is a complete test or
data generation cycle:

1   production of a removable volume of software;

2   off-line tests or data generation, perhaps on a
    different and disconnected site;

3   uploading of the test or generation results;

4   analysis on the development host;

Iterations

So far, we have stressed the logical sequencing
of the four steps leading to (a first approximation to) the
project guide. Almost inevitably, iterations of these steps
will become necessary, as indicated for the last step.

In this respect, there is a strong analogy
between the life cycle model for the development methods and
this planning and organisation model. The logical sequencing
is the overall method but it does not guarantee immediate
success.

Figure 3.3 summarises possible iterations and
indicates in parentheses the reasons for making them. These
iterations affect the data base entities describing tasks,

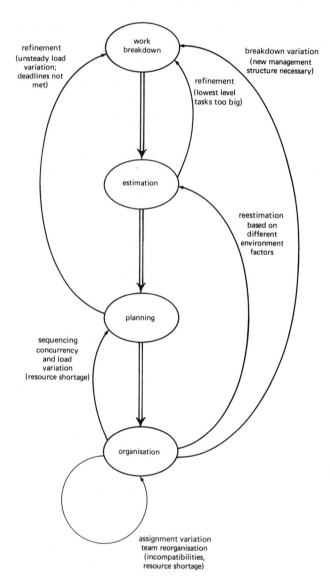

Figure 3.3   Project management activities and their iteration

persons, teams and resources. In order to keep these entities under change and configuration control, management documents are considered products in the context of our Configuration Control method. It is therefore possible to keep the iterations of these products in the data base during the iterative process of generating the Project Guide. Management may choose a specific configuration which need not be the last one developed. Furthermore, it is possible to record the evolution of tools, persons, tasks, and resources over the life time of the project, and of teams, persons and resources over a longer time period comprising several projects.

The following table shows how the product structure can be exploited in order to differentiate between the different types of changes. It shows for which changes in relationships or attributes of atomic data items of the products new versions, editions or iterations may be generated.

for the PRODUCT	Creation of a new		
	VERSION	EDITION	ITERATION
	for a change of		
TASK	Description	. Persons . Products	All other attributes and relationships
PERSON	Project	. Team location . Position in hierarchy	. Assignments . Task responsibilities . Team responsibility
TEAM	Project	. Persons . Leader	. Cost . Availability . Resources
RESOURCE	Project	. Teams . Tasks	. Cost . Availability

Using the controlled deletion process of the configuration control system, all unwanted configurations generated during the planning and organisation process can be eliminated.

The products for which the largest number of iterations will be produced are tasks. Whenever their status is examined by management and the effort used updated new iterations should be produced. The history of these iterations will contain complete references to resources/persons and products to which the tasks are linked, at the time of the generation of the new iterations. Consequently each task iteration captures an accurate snapshot of the task progress.

The histories of the iterations of the products of type person, team and resource contain (incomplete) references to persons, teams, resources and tasks.

3.2.2.2.3 Project Control

Project control is based on the current project guide. Progress is monitored by collecting data reflecting the current project state and relating them to the effort, cost and schedule data predicted in the project guide. Deviations which indicate that the project will not stay within time and budget may lead to an updated project guide, or some remedial action such as the reallocation of resources.

Progress Monitoring

One can imagine numerous ways of collecting data. Data about the state of a task and the effort used on it can be associated with the tasks in the project chart at regular intervals, for instance on a weekly basis. These data can be fed in by the person(s), who is (are) assigned the tasks, and to a certain degree verified by statistical data automatically gathered which show how often generation procedures have been run for the products linked to the tasks.

Furthermore, the consistency of all the data collected can be checked by summing the effort used over all the tasks assigned to a person and a team, and comparing them to the resources which have been available.

Relating these data to the predicted data in the project chart may reveal deviations. If the lowest level tasks require little effort over a short period of time then schedule and budget overruns for these tasks should become visible early enough to allow the management team to take corrective actions.

However, if the tasks are large (limit: the project), generally the remedy will come too late to bring the project back onto budget and time limits.

It is therefore important to have methods by which the current state of a product can be related to its anticipated final state. Such methods are only possible if the products are developed according to specific methods which are related to each other in an overall life cycle method. This is a strong point for the use of a coherent programming support environment.

Coherent development methods will allow one to assess the size and complexity of a document under development and to compare these attributes with the estimated size and complexity which led to the current plan. The resultant ratio can be compared with an estimate of the percentage of the work done provided by the person working on the task of producing the document. This ratio can reveal a deviation from the planned budget and timescales very early on. The failure to complete a task as planned can thus be anticipated and not merely revealed once it has happened.

Corrective Actions

Corrective management actions are not only triggered by deviations or tendencies towards deviations but also by the results of periodical validations of the current Project Guide with respect to the existing system representations. Even if these representations have been produced according to the plans their semantic contents may indicate that subsequent representations may be more voluminous and complex than anticipated when generating the current project guide.

In any case, determining the appropriate corrective actions is again a delicate management task. The management team generally has many options. The effect of each of these options on the project guide has to be studied. This is done by iterating any step of project planning and organisation as described above. If the option is to change the project objectives in the sense that the requirements expression is changed then the impact of this change has to be assessed with respect to the documents already existing. Here the inter-document relationships across life-cycle levels are exploited in order to localise areas of change. The volume and complexity of these areas provide the basis for the estimation of the change effort.

Finally, maintenance actions can be seen as mini projects for which a project guide is set up in the same way as for a full scale development project. The work performed in a maintenance project will change documents pertaining to the system under consideration. Generally, the change at the place where the trouble is located propagates both to the left and to the right in the levels of representation in the life cycle model.

3.2.2.2.4 Integration and Quality Management

In this section on project management, we have used the terms management, project manager, team and person while speaking of the people involved in a project. The discussion so far has not dealt with a specific organisation for the people in a production context or on a specific project. In fact, our data model allows for arbitrary graphs of entities and relationships and could equally well be used to describe project, functional or matrix types of organisations as discussed in [Dalby (1980)].

However, we want to give an interpretation of the intermediate management levels corresponding to the tasks between the root task and the lowest-level tasks. Since the recursive task structure seems to fit the life cycle model and the system structure it should also match the organisational structure.

This match can be achieved by viewing the intermediate tasks as the tasks of integration and quality management (IQM). Due to the task hierarchy it is natural that tasks on a higher level be concerned with the "integration" of the results of tasks on a lower level. Integration implies delivery and acceptance, and hence quality control.

By giving this interpretation to middle management we attribute to it the configuration control role in our method.

IQM has the authority and responsibility to:

1   control the system generation chain, regeneration mechanisms and system parameterisation;

2   control the development organisation, i.e. the use of standard tools;

3   manage the archives of the various system releases;

4   control the use of defined interfaces between subsystems.

All these functions are supported by our configuration control method by means of generation procedures and access and visibility control through libraries and product bases. Again, a strong point for the coherence of the APSE.

Besides the above functions, integration and quality management must:

1   impose Quality Controls before accepting an internal delivery;

2   perform integration testing, i.e. coordinate the simultaneous validation and verification of (all) the software subsystems or documents;

3   validate system releases;

4   develop the necessary test plans and control
    procedures.

All these functions require an intimate
technical knowledge of the system to be developed as well as
of the development methods.

IQM offers itself therefore as the driving force
behind trouble shooting and change processing. Without
bothering top management, IQM may initiate fault finding and
investigation, and schedule and drive the implementation of
minor changes. Since IQM manages the archives of system
releases as the configuration control authority, it has an
important role in the maintenance phase of a project, too.
Figure 3.4 illustrates the basic relationships between
project management, IQM, and development.

We will now discuss IQM methods in more detail.

A Specific Method of Integration

In the usual sense of the term, integration
covers the coordination activities between the
implementation and testing of the software subsystems
constituting a given system. However, integration in a more
general sense may be any activity of coordination involving
the "fusion" of several parts into a whole. Integration thus
may also help bring together parts of a requirements
expression, system specification or abstract functional
specification which have been developed by different persons
or teams. However, on these levels in the life cycle,
integration is much simpler since far fewer bits and pieces
are involved. In the implementation, the number of different
components which have to be managed by an integration team
may well go into the thousands for large systems. We
concentrate the discussion therefore mainly on this phase.

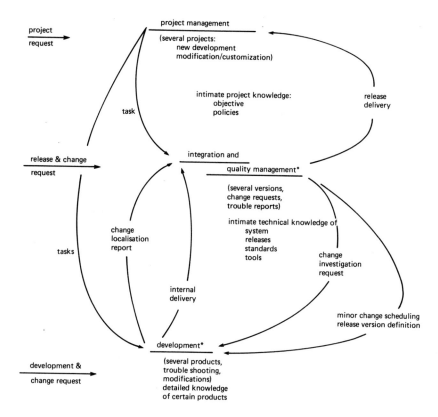

* may have subordinate teams

Figure 3.4   Basic relationships involving integration and quality management

The Organisation

We assume that on a large project the work is done by several teams each with a different function. There are most likely to be a specification team, a design team, and several development teams carrying out implementation work. In such a project environment, IQM should be taken care of by an integration team. This team is in charge of constructing predefined "releases" and carrying out the test plans on these systems prior to release. Due to this role, the IQM team should also be responsible for providing the development teams with the necessary production environment for the target releases. This production environment consists primarily of a set of production tools (e.g. compilers, cross-compilers, V&V tools,...) and a set of common references for the development teams (e.g. a simulated target system environment for unit testing, a reference release as the common start point, interface descriptions, specification and design documents,...).

This environment can be set up with the help of the configuration control method which allows the IQM team to define generation procedures, access rights and library visibility.

In practice, integration may be performed on various levels by a hierarchy of integration teams (partial or progressive integration, internal reviews, partial deliveries). In this way, the integration task may be implemented more smoothly. Again the visibility of products between the development teams can be managed so that some form of "information hiding" and "separation of concerns" can be achieved. Figure 3.5 illustrates the organisation.

In this organisation, the test and validation burden can be divided into:

1 unit testing, performed on each software subsystem by a development team, in a limited environment according to test plans reviewed by the IQM team;

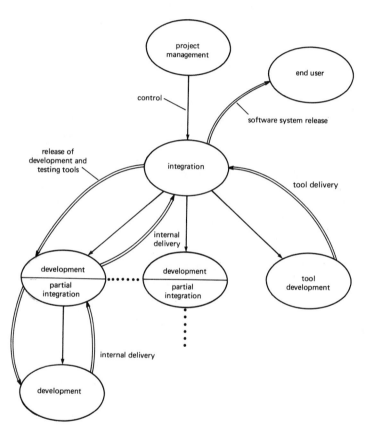

Figure 3.5   Schema of control and data flow for a demanding project

2   software   integration   testing,   performed   on   a
complete   version   of   a   software   system   by   the
integration team, possibly using a simulated test
environment;

3   system verification, performed by the end user on
the   basis   of   the   requirements   expression and
system   specification,   preferably   in   the   real
operating environment.

Integration Products

The   roles   and   functions   in   a   project
organisation   are   embodied   in   tasks   and their associated
products   which are kept under configuration control (access
rights/visibility).

A   specific   set   of products is associated with
the tasks of IQM. They can be classified as:

1   "sys" (for system) products

2   "subsys" (for subsystem) products

3   "site" (for user-site) products

Configuration control has to have a knowledge of
the   structure of these products which are either predefined
in   the   APSE,   or   more   likely,   defined   by   the   project
management and IQM so that they are tailored to the specific
needs of the project.

These   products group together several documents
which   have   predictably   similar   evolution   rhythms   and
patterns.   The follow up activities on these documents then
are   well-defined   and   may   play   a   key   role   in   the
organisation.

Products   of   the   above   mentioned   types   can
identify a release (name/version number) in various ways:

1   Sys   product data includes

1.1   complete references to all the source code and the executable system representation (binary or intermediate form) of a reference system

1.2   a list of all the subsystems making up the software, with relative "visibility rights"

2   Subsys   product data includes

2.1   a list of all the desired components of the subsystem (the term "components" may mean the set of modules, or Ada libraries, etc.)

2.2   a list of all the components actually available together with their complete names.

3   Site   product data includes

3.1   a list of sys reference products

3.2   a list of added components which correspond to replacement versions of software already available in the relevant sys product, or to entirely new components to be added to these products.

3.3   a set of site-dependent product descriptions.

A site product is used for each explicit site dependent delivery. The site dependent product description may, for example, indicate how a tape or a disk or a PROM has to be produced for the purpose of testing in a simulated environment. The site product may use the "simulated system" as sys reference product, and as added components the software to be tested, and the test data.

A formal delivery also involves a site product. In this case, the site product is "owned" by the integration team. The name of the release to be delivered is the (only) element in the sys reference product list.

A sys product is created when a new line of releases is prepared. At the same time a subsystem decomposition is provided which gives rise to the creation of subsys products. A new iteration of these products is generated by collecting all the software documents referenced, from subsystems.

It may seem that sys, subsys and site products are redundant concepts given the task structure and its relation with products. This is true if the integration products contain only documents which are produced by the tasks underneath the integration task. However, this is hardly ever the case since many components of a release may be reused in which case there is no task for developing these components. Therefore, these integration products are clearly contributing to the power and flexibility of IQM.

The responsibilities of IQM may be defined in terms of these products and specific operations on the products. For instance, to redeliver an old release means recollecting all the products and their components referenced indirectly by a sys-product iteration corresponding to the release through the subsys-product iterations corresponding to the release.

In order to function properly, IQM needs all the functions offered by the Configuration Control System. The most important ones are:

1 a precise identification of each and every software component (whether tool or document)

2 easy access to any specific component

3 the possibility of listing all the software components directly or indirectly involved in the generation of a given (sub)system.

4   the   need   to maintain at any given time, several
versions   of   a   (sub)system   with varying access
rights.

Quality Control
        Quality   Control   in   the sense of verifying the
coherence   of   all   the   parts of a system and deciding that
nothing   is   missing,   is   automatically   performed   by   our
methods   of   configuration   control   and   integration.   The
application   of   standards and norms and the use of standard
tools   are   also   controlled   by   configuration   control   by
installing generation procedures specific to product types.
        Furthermore V&V methods are inherent in the APSE
which   we   have outlined and these guarantee product quality
in   the   sense   of   conformity   with   the   requirements   and
internal consistency.
        Quality   control in the sense of design and code
quality   or   complexity   analysis   may,   in   addition,   be
performed by IQM with the help   of   methods and tools, along
the lines of those reported in [Miller (1979)].

3.2.2.3   Satisfaction of Requirements
        The methods largely satisfy the requirements set
out in section 2.5, so we will   not   discuss satisfaction of
requirements in detail here. Instead we briefly consider the
satisfaction   of   requirements   for   coherence   between   the
methods.
        The project management methods are coherent with
the   development   and   configuration   control   methods
essentially   because   they   are   based   on   a common product
model.   Coherence   with the development methods is obviously
essential   and   this topic is treated by means of an example
in section 3.3.
        Coherence with the configuration control methods
helps satisfy the requirements for:

1   Controlling and monitoring the evolution of the
    project guide as the parts of the project guide
    are held in the database and subject to
    configuration control in the same way as the
    products of the development methods.

2   Enforcing   standards   through   generation
    procedures.

3   Integration management through the concepts of
    library visibility and site specific products.

3.2.2.4 Alternative Methods

Although management methods   have   only   been
described at an overview level they are clearly quite
complex, and they are strongly dependent on the
configuration control method. Simpler alternative methods
could be produced, for example by amalgamating the product
and task concepts, but with consequent loss in flexibility
and generality. This being the case we believe it to be more
appropriate to consider alternative methods for "filling in
the detail" within our overall framework, rather than
alternatives to our framework.

A number of detailed management methods exist,
e.g. those reported in [Boehm (1976) and Reifer (1979)] and
chief programmer teams. All of these methods can be
incorporated into our framework.   The   most important
criterion for judging these methods is how well they fit in
with the configuration control methods, both from the point
of view of being controllable by, and being coherent with,
the configuration control method. The former is quite easy
to satisfy because of the generality of the configuration
control method. Surprisingly it is quite rare to have this
sort of coherence, and, as Boehm [Boehm (1976)] puts it,
management methods are usually "decoupled from software
technology".

The final point of importance is that it must be

possible to set up particular management methods required for a particular project, within the overall framework. This implies considerable flexibility within the MAPSE database and the management tools. We return to this point in section 3.4.1.

3.2.2.5 Enhancements and Extensions

The topic of project management is clearly quite difficult and several design iterations will be needed before a truly satisfactory method can be developed. Particular methods, e.g. estimation techniques, and automatic event-driven communication would have to be elaborated in detail. Considerable emphasis would have to be put on "meta-methods" and techniques for adaptation of particular methods to specific needs.

3.3   Coherence of the Methods

3.3.1   Introduction

We have considered the individual Development and Management Methods more or less in isolation. To show that they can be used as the basis for a coherent APSE we need to consider how these methods can be integrated. In particular we need to know how easy or difficult it is to perform the transformations and checks between the representations, and how well the Development Methods integrate with the Management Methods.

To this end we consider one iteration round the whole development cycle. First we discuss the checks that have to be made between the representations, then we consider what happens when we make a change to the requirement and follow the consequences of the change through to the Module Code. This discussion is based on two of the documents from our experiment, viz [Systems Designers Limited (1982g)] which discusses the checks which have to be made on the transformations between the representations and [Systems Designers Limited (1982h)] which considers the effect on all the representations of making a change in the requirement.

3.3.2   A Development Cycle

3.3.2.1   Introduction

We consider first the checks on the validity of the transformstions between the representations. We will not discuss the check on the "transformation" to produce the RE as this has been covered in section 3.1.2.

3.3.2.2   Requirement Expression to System Specification

The check on the RE to SS transformation is essentially a plausibility check, rather than a demonstration of equivalence, as the SS notation contains considerabley more information than the RE and the RE is somewhat imprecise.

We have to show that the RWAI and the LODI in the SS match the inputs and outputs in the RE. There will

often be a one to one correspondence between the
representations, but some data flows in one representation
may be combined in another. Checks must be made to show that
the LODI and RWAI contain at least as much information as
their counterparts in the RE.

Checks have to be made on the equivalence of the
functions in the SS and the activities in the RE. This is an
informal check showing that the transfer characteristic in
the SS is compatible with the prose description in the RE.
The ADI in the SS will not necessarily have counterparts in
the RE, but their influence will have to be taken into
consideration when checking the equivalence of activities in
the RE and functions in the SS.

Finally the data item to device mappings in the
SS have to be checked against the viewpoint hierarchy in the
RE (this has not been done in [Systems Designers Limited
(1982g)]).

3.3.2.3 System Specification to Abstract Functional Specification

The SS to AFS transformation is difficult to
check in that the transformation (a design process) may
produce quite complex relationships between the functions
and data items in the two representations. This difficulty
is to some extent ameliorated by the fact that the SS and
AFS are couched in essentially similar representations.

The RWAI and LODI in the SS should have direct
equivalents in the AFS. The mappings may not be one to one,
as, for example, one logical output may appear on a number
of physical devices, and hence may appear several times in
the AFS. The relationship between the ADI in the SS and IDI
in the AFS may be more complex, as the internal structure of
the system may differ quite significantly from the external
view of the system presented in the SS.

Showing functional equivalence between the two
representations involves showing that the composition of the
AFS functions yields equivalent transfer characteristics to
those of the functions in the SS. At present this operation

is informal, but we believe that it will be possible to extend the notation for the AFS so that the checks can be made more formal. It should be noted that it would be very valuable to formalise, and perhaps automate, this check because of the difficulty of producing good designs and the low probability of being able to (even partially) automate the design process.

3.3.2.4 Abstract Functional Specification to Module Specification

The AFS to MS transformation again involves a change in notation. However the mapping between the objects in the two notations is fairly straightforward so that it should be easy to see which parts of the representations correspond. The MS will in general contain more detail than the AFS but we should in principle be able to show that the two representations are equivalent.

We need to show that the types and data objects in the MS are capable of representing the information contained in the data items in the AFS. Thus we need to check the correlation between the Ada/ANNA annotations and the syntactic notation used in the AFS.

To show functional "equivalence" we have to check that the AFS transfer characteristics are accurately represented by the ANNA annotations for the corresponding subprograms in the MS. There is a clear structural equivalence between the ANNA subprogram annotations and the AFS tables, so this check should be quite straightforward once the correlation between the data items has been established.

3.3.2.5 Module Design and Module Code

For the remaining representations we have the task of showing the validity of a set of transformations within the combined Ada/ANNA notation, and without any major structural reorganisations in the representations. This is comparatively straightforward informally, but becomes more difficult if we wish to make the verification formal. In this case program proving techniques and tools become necessary.

3.3.2.6 Management

The management methods have been described in considerable detail in section 3.2. The management methods are based on the life-cycle model and on the representations required to support the chosen development methods. It should therefore be evident from the description in section 3.2 that the two sets of methods are coherent, so this topic will not be discussed in detail here.

There are, however, two important points which are worth repeating:

1 Project management is responsible for planning, initiating and controlling the transformation and verification activities on the basis of the project guide.

2 Configuration control records the history of all the products resulting from these activities, and guarantees that each activity operates on a consistent set of products.

A detailed example of the relationship between the representations and the configuration control mechanisms is given in Annex 2 "A general data model for software development and maintenance". This annex describes how the representations from the development methods fit into the product structure defined by SDL2020.

3.3.2.7 Summary

In general the validation activities are quite difficult to perform. The two major causal factors are the fact that many of the mappings between the representations are complex, and the notations used for the different representations are dissimilar. These factors are amply illustrated even by the outline of the checking process

given in [Systems Designers Limited (1982g)]. We believe
that these factors are inherent to the task, and do not
reflect deficiencies in the methods or representations.
However it is hard to assess whether or not the degree to
which these problems arise is worse than necessary due to a
poor choice of the combination of methods.

3.3.3   Change Processing
3.3.3.1   Introduction

We can see how amenable the overall development
method is to handling changes by considering the affects of
a change in the RE on the other representations in the
model. In our experiment [Systems Designers Limited (1982h)]
we simply specified that one activity which had been
performed outside the system should now be performed by the
system. This change affects all the other representations
including the Module Code. The changes to the
representations and the effects on project management and
configuration control are briefly discussed below.

3.3.3.2   Requirement Expression

The change does not affect the Operational
Requirement (the description of the system and it's
environment). An extra activity and some associated data
flows are required in the part of the RE which corresponds
to the System Specification.

3.3.3.3   System Specification

This change in the RE is matched by an extra
function and some extra LODI, RWAI and ADI in the SS.
Additionally the structure of some of the existing data
items are affected. The correspondence between the data
items in the RE and SS make it clear which items in the SS
have to be reconsidered. It is therefore easy to see what
affect the change has on the SS.

3.3.3.4   Abstract Functional Specification

The changes to the LODI and RWAI in the SS are

carried over directly into the AFS. Additional data items
are required in the AFS corresponding to the ADI in the SS.
The additional function in the SS is implemented by
extending the functionality of one of the functions in the
AFS.

3.3.3.5 Module Specification, Design and Code

There is a direct correspondence between the
data items in the AFS and MS, and similarly between the
functions in the AFS and subprograms in the MS, hence it is
easy to carry the change into the MS and subsequent
representations.

3.3.3.6 Project Management

Change processing affects project management
differently depending on the magnitude and scope of the
change. These factors can be assessed by considering the
relationships between the atomic data items in the
representations.

Changes which have a significant impact, such as
the change described above, will have to be treated as small
development projects and planned and controlled by the
project management team.

Less major changes, e.g. a simple "bug fix" can
usually be handled by means of pre-defined change control
protocols as described in section 3.2.2. In either case the
well-defined representations and development methods
facilitate the task of change management.

3.3.3.7 Configuration Control

One of the main raisons d'etre for a
configuration control method is the need to preserve the
consistency of a software system which is subject to change.
The configuration control method described in section 3.2.1
supports the processing of changes in various ways by means
of the four level product structure.

Small changes such as simple revisions to
modules may only lead to a new product iteration being

produced by the invocation of an existing generation procedure. Larger changes may lead to the generation of a new product, or a new version or edition of an existing product by the invocation of a (potentially new) generation procedure. In either case, the "derivation history" of the new product is recorded.

The configuration control method provides a way of verifying whether a given product is built using specific, for example the most recent, iterations of constituent products. By using this facility the extent to which a change has to be propagated can be assessed, e.g. if the Abstract Functional Specification has been revised, then the Module Specification produced on the basis of the preceeding iteration of the AFS will have to be reviewed and probably updated.

The change propagation described above is occurring at the macroscopic level, and is fairly easy to control. It would probably be desirable to to exploit the relationships between atomic data items to direct attention to the appropriate part of a representation when propagating changes. Unfortunately it is difficult to implement a system which does exploit the relationships between the atomic data items, and this problem is discussed in Annex 3. At present, therefore, relationships between atomic data items will be regarded as being merely a convenient form of documentation, and not the basis for change propagation.

The configuration control method described in section 3.2 allows changes to be made to representations in the same way that the representations were produced in the first place. Thus change processing is seen as an iteration of the development process, thus there is a very strong degree of coherence between the overall development method and the method of configuration control.

3.3.3.8 Summary

It is quite easy to see which items in any one representation should be reconsidered (or added) because of a change in the preceeding representation. Although our experience comes from only one small experiment we believe it is generally easy to find the consequences of a change because of the fairly clear relationships between the objects in the representations in any pair of "adjacent" levels.

This ease of determining which items are to be changed aids project management, as it is easy to generate new plans and to see what the effect is on the configuration of the product being produced. These benefits exist even when relationships between representations are retained at only a macroscopic level, but greater benefits would accrue from the availability of relationships at the microscopic level.

3.3.4 Gaps and Overlaps

There are surprisingly few serious gaps or overlaps between the methods and representations which we have studied in our experiment. Most of the gaps are caused by shortcomings in individual representations, e.g. the difficulty of showing functional composition in the AFS, and the inability of ANNA to deal with tasking. Most of the potential overlaps, e.g. between CORE and the A-7 techniques [Systems Designers Limited (1982b)] can be resolved within the existing methods simply by adding extra rules delimiting the scope of the individual methods.

3.3.5 Summary

The methods investigated are surprisingly well integrated considering that they were all developed in widely differing environments. From the point of view of showing the relationships between the representations the Development Methods are all quite compatible. This means that it is quite possible to store the representations within the same database and to record relationships between the representations. The methods could become even better integrated if it were possible to record relationships between objects on a microscopic level.

The whole spectrum of the development process is

covered with sufficient flexibility that the number of
levels of representation can be adjusted to suit the size of
the project.

The "product based" Management Methods are
sufficiently general to be able to integrate with, and
control, the Development Methods which we have investigated.

Automation of the transformations between the
representations, or automation of the validation of these
processes, will be very difficult for most of the methods.
We can not be certain to what extent this difficulty is
inherent, and to what extent it reflects the choice of an
awkward combination of methods or notations.

3.4   Implementing an APSE

3.4.1   The MAPSE Data Model

Much of the discussion of the management methods has been based on a specific view of the data model used in the development and maintenance of software systems. This specific view is illustrated by the general data model in Annex 2, and by the microscopic views of some of the representations in Annex 3.

These data models are intended to be illustrative, not definitive. The notation chosen is derived from that developed for the SDS database [RSRE (undated)] which is a simple entity relationship model where the relationships may not carry attributes.

It is not expected that the data model would be implemented directly as described in Annex 2. For example if it were to be implemented in the KAPSE database currently under development for the CEC by Olivetti the model would be transformed and could be made considerably simpler. This is illustrated by Figure 3.6 which gives an example of how the abstract data model might be recast into an implementable schema.

An important issue concerning the data model is its modifiability and extensibility. Different organisations may want to implement different methods in their APSEs. The schema should therefore be easily modifiable, or ideally, it should be possible to generate the schema automatically from some higher level representation, e.g a definition of the transfer characteristics of the set of APSE tools. It is beyond the scope of this study to consider these topics in any detail. However the ESPRIT [ESPRIT (1982)] study "Software Production and Maintenance Management System (SPMMS)" will have to address this issue, and it may also address that of achieving configuration control over atomic data items.

3.4.2   Support Tools

We will not attempt to give an exhaustive list of tools which could be produced to support the methods

Figure 3.6   Data model

which we advocate as part of a coherent APSE, but we will
indicate the range and type of tools which we think would be
useful in an integrated APSE. We classify tools in a number
of ways, including the level of support which they give, and
whether or not they can be produced with "existing
technology".

There are a number of different ways of
classifying support tools. One basic classification is
whether the tool is aimed at directly supporting the
development process, i.e. it automates a transformation or
verification, or it is ancillary to the development process,
e.g. a performance analysis tool. We will primarily be
concerned with tools which support the development process,
and management functions, but we will mention some ancillary
tools. The distinction between these two classes of tool
should be obvious.

Another important classification is whether the
tool is passive, e.g. checking a representation to see if it
is consistent, or active, e.g. prompting for information to
make a representation complete, based on an analysis of the
representation. Clearly the active tools are more difficult
to produce than the passive tools, but they may be
particularly valuable, particularly in aiding Requirement
Expression and System Specification. In the following
discussion tools can be assumed to be passive, unless we
state otherwise.

The main classification which we will use in
describing the tools is level of support. We distinguish
three levels:

Basic   clerical support for syntax checking and
            recording the representations; minimal management
            support;

Aggregated basic, plus tool support for completeness and
            consistency checks within each representation;
            management support for planning, progress
            monitoring and configuration control;

Integrated aggregated, plus tool support for checks between
representations and perhaps with tools for
performing automated transformation between
representations; estimation tools etc. for the
management activities.

We describe the tools by means of three tables,
one for each of the three levels of support identified
above. Within the tables we identify each tool with a
(hopefully) meaningful name. We also summarise the levels of
representation to which it is pertinent, and give some
information on the ease with which the tool could be
implemented.

We indicate both the representation(s) to which
the tool gives support (either in the generation or
subsequent analysis of the representation), and the
representations which the tool requires in order to perform
its job. We denote the individual representations by their
mnemonics, RE, SS, etc., and "each" is used to mean each
representation individually, and "all" is used to mean some,
or possibly all, representations simultaneously. Finally we
indicate support to the management activities by the
mnemonic "Man".

In considering implementability, we state
whether or not the tool can be built using "existing
technology", to our knowledge, and indicate which "meta -
tools" might be useful in producing the tools. If we say
that a tool can be built using existing technology, this
means that we know of a tool which works with our, or a very
similar representaion. We give references for the less
common tools. The references are given indirectly because of
lack of space in the tables. The full references are
presented after the third table. The "meta - tools" covers
both tools for building tools, e.g. parser generators, and
simple tools which could be incorporated into more
sophisticated tools.

We mention the following meta - tools by their

abbreviations:

Parser Generator (or compiler compiler) - Parser Gen.

Database Traversal Tool, driven from DB schema - DB trav

Database input facilities - DB input

Database output facilities - QL

          For some tools a parser generator, a database
traversal tool or even a Query Language processor might be
appropriate, depending on whether information is stored in
textual form or as a set of related objects in the database.
Where there is this choice we specify which tool we think to
be most likely to be appropriate.
          In all the tables we assume that the basic MAPSE
faciltities are available. We consider the basic level of
support first:

BASIC SUPPORT

Tool	Support	Based on	Existing Technol.	Meta - Tool
Syntax Checker	Each	Each	Yes	Parser Gen.
Syntax Directed Editor	Each	Each	Yes, eg [1]	Parser Gen.
Report Generators	Each + Man	Each+ Man	Yes	DB trav.

AGGREGATED TOOLS

Tool	Support	Based On	Existing Technol.	Meta – Tool
Consistency and Completeness Checker	Each + Man	Each + Man	Yes, eg [2]	DB trav.
Program Analysers eg Control & Data Flow	Mainly MS, MD, MC	Mainly MS, MD, MC	Yes, eg [3]	Parser Gen.
Standards Enforcer	Each	Each	Yes, eg prepro-cessors	Parser Gen.
PERT/ Critical Path Analyser	Man	Man	Yes	–
Interactive Update tool for project management info.	Man	Man	No	DB Trav.
Progress Monitoring and reporting	Man	Man	No	–
Management Reporting Path Definition	Man	Man	Yes [4]	DB input
"Browsing" Tool	All + Man	All + Man	No	DB Trav.
Configuration Control Nucleus	Man	Man	Yes, eg [5]	DB input
System Regenerator – Top Down/ Bottom Up	All + Man	All + Man	Yes, eg [5]	DB Trav.
Archiving	All + Man	All + Man	Yes, eg [5]	DB Trav.
Change Identification and Propagation	All + Man	All + Man	Yes for macro. view	DB Trav.
Graphical I/O	All + Man	All + Man	Yes	–

INTEGRATED SUPPORT

Tool	Support	Based On	Existing Technol.	Meta - Tool
Transformation Driver (Active)	Each	Each	Yes, eg [6]	Parser Gen.
Modelling/ Simulation Performance Analysis	AFS,MS	SS,AFS, MS	Yes, survey [7]	-
Rapid Implementation	MS, MD	MS, MD	Yes, eg [2]	-
Symbolic Execution	MD	MD	Yes, eg [2]	-
Rapid prototyping	AFS, MS	AFS, MS	Only specific appl. domains	-
Program Prover (Active)	MS, MD, MC	MS, MD, MC	Yes, eg [8]	-
Estimation and Statistical Analysis	Man	Each + Man	Yes for code, eg [9]	DB Trav.
Work Breakdown Tool (Active) to aid in human task allocation	Man	Man + Each	No	-

Indirect References

[1]	[Teichrow and Hershey (1977)]
[2]	[Cheatham (1981)]
[3]	[Fosdick and Osterweil (1976)]
[4]	[Cashman and Holt (1980)]
[5]	[Maissonneuve et al (1981)]
[6]	[Partsch and Steinbruggen (1981)]
[7]	[Miller (1979)]
[8]	[Good (1977)]
[9]	[Keller (1979)]

Although some of the tools we have mentioned above are not based on "existing technology" we have tried to avoid highly futuristic tools which are unlikely to be implementable within the forseeable future. Having said this, there is a clear gradation in implementation difficulty from the basic support level to the integrated level.

3.4.3 Summary

We have outlined a data model which could be constructed using the facilities of the KAPSE data base to support the methods which we have investigated. In section 3.4.2 above we have identified a number of tools, most of which can be produced using existing "tool technology", which would give varying levels of support for the methods we have studied.

Thus we may conclude that it will be technically feasible to build an APSE based on existing methods once a MAPSE is available. Chapter 4 discusses the difficulty and cost of producing APSEs of varying levels of sophistication, and thus addresses the question of the economic feasibility of producing an APSE.

4
Conclusions and recommendations

4.1 Introduction

We believe that our study has given some
valuable evidence on the viability of producing a coherent
methodology which can be supported in an APSE, and on the
benefits of using such an APSE. However the scale of the
experimental work which we have been able to perform during
this study, coupled with the lack of any substantial
comparison of methods, means that our conclusions are
inevitably somewhat subjective and limited in certain
respects. Nonetheless we believe that the evidence which we
have produced is sufficiently conclusive to justify
performing more extensive studies to try to produce an APSE
design based on existing methods and known implementation
techniques. We shall be arguing these points in the
following three sections, concluding with an outline of a
development plan for a coherent APSE.

As a general point we believe that tool support
for methods is critical. The reason for this is that the
clerical overhead of producing and maintaining the
representations required by the methods is substantial. This
overhead will mitigate against the use of the methods
regardless of the benefits of having the representations
kept accurate and up to date. Worse, the effort required to
check the consistency and completeness of any representation
is large, and typically grows faster than linearly with the
size of the representation. There is little benefit in
producing representations unless we can check them and gain
some confidence in their validity. Thus we believe that tool
support, at least at the level of clerical support and

consistency and completeness checking, is essential if the methods are to be successfully used for large projects. We will assume that this level of support is available when considering the benefits of using the APSE in the next section.

4.2 Benefits of Using the APSE

We have been investigating a coherent APSE giving support to all stages of the Development Process and to Project Management. Consequently we will be assessing the benefits of using such an APSE by comparison with using a set of isolated methods, perhaps supported by isolated tools, but not integrated with project management methods in a coherent environment. In other words we are trying to assess the "add on benefits" of having coherent development support, linked to project management facilities.

A major benefit to the Project Management team is that we have Project Visibility as it is clear which representations have to be produced in developing the system. This clear identification of products, in the general sense, gives a strong link between the development methods and project management methods. This aids in the provision of project control as the planning and progress monitoring can be based on the actual representations being produced, rather than on the (perhaps rather optimistic) reports from the development staff. If the granularity of the products is kept small then the degree of control which can be achieved is high. The corollary of this is that we should have early detection of problems, thereby giving the opportunity to take corrective action before too much slip has occurred. Thus the second major benefit is that we have the potential for better project control.

On the development side there are a number of benefits. First we have a set of representations at varying levels of abstraction which enable the system developer more readily to master the system complexity. Further these representations cover all aspects of the Development Process, with conceptually simple transformations between the levels. This means that the system developer can perform his primary task, that of designing and building the system, without having to bridge enormous gaps between the representations, or being sidetracked into developing extra notations or methods in order to fill these gaps.

Second the system developer can have much more

confidence in the correctness, of the representations he is producing as the consistency and completeness of the representations can be checked. Further there is the potential for checking or aiding in performing the transformation between the representations. This gives the system developer higher confidence in the accuracy of the succession of transformations from requirements to executable system, hence in the "correctness" of the system being produced.

If we consider the ease of making changes to the system then we can see that there are benefits both for the development and management teams. From the development point of view, once we have identified the item to be changed in a particular representation then we can find all the other items which we need to consider by "following" the relationships between the representations. Clearly this will also guide the management team in deciding which new tasks have to be planned. Thus the maintenance, as well as the development, team will benefit from the provision of a coherent APSE.

From the point of view of providing tool support within the APSE, we have the capability of producing more tools within a coherent APSE because we can automate the transformations, or the checking of the transformations between the representations. Further since all the tools will use a common database it will probably be possible to produce a number of general purpose tools, and to produce some "meta - tools" (e.g. for database traversal) to aid in the production of representation - specific tools.

The above benefits follow more or less directly from the coherence, and complete Life Cycle coverage, of the APSE. There are two other important benefits which we believe would accrue from the use of a coherent APSE, but for which we can produce no real substantiating evidence. These benefits are that the systems produced will be more reliable, and the Life Cycle costs will be lower, than they would have been without coherent support.

Our experiment gave little evidence in these

areas except that certain problems were found during
requirements analysis which only appeared during coding when
the system had previously been built. The only direct way of
producing conclusive evidence on these two benefits is to
perform an experiment, or a series thereof, covering the
whole Life Cycle of a substantial software product. Apart
from the cost of such an exercise there are technical
problems, such as the difficulty of performing a control
experiment, which make this form of experiment seem
unattractive. Thus there is a very genuine difficulty in
establishing the cost-effectiveness of a coherent APSE.
However the Application Area Projects funded under the
extension to the CECs Multi-Annual Data Processing Programme
may at least partially resolve this problem.

It is unlikely that evidence about the
cost-effectiveness of coherent methods will be available for
some time. However it is worth observing that the onus of
proof should be on those who disbelieve in the value of
coherent methodologies and toolsets to show that an
undisciplined, incoherent, approach to software development
is cost-effective! Consequently it is sensible to proceed in
trying to develop coherent methodologies and toolsets even
though substantive evidence of their value is not yet
available.

Returning to the more tangible benefits of using
an APSE, it should be stressed that a coherent APSE will
benefit the customer for a product, as well as the developer
of the product. The customer will have higher confidence
than he would otherwise have had that the system being built
will satisfy his requirements, and that it will be built to
the agreed timescale and cost.

In summary we can see that there are a
significant number of major technical and managerial
benefits of using an APSE based on coherent development and
management methodologies. It is to be hoped that the
Application Area Projects mentioned above will go some way
towards establishing the cost-effectiveness of using a
coherent APSE.

4.3 Technical Feasibility of using the APSE

We are concerned here primarily with the range of applications for which a coherent APSE, based on a given set of methods, could be used.

We can only really assess the generality of an APSE given knowledge of the specific set of methods and tools incorporated within the APSE. We very briefly make the assessment for an APSE based on the techniques which we have investigated, as an illustration of the type of assessment which would have to be made for any proposed APSE development.

CORE has already been used on a wide variety of projects, and is capable of describing human, as well as automated systems. We believe therefore that it is of very high generality, and that it would not form the limiting factor in the generality of a coherent APSE.

The A-7 techniques as initially described [Heninger et al (1978)] were fairly limited in terms of the types of data which they could describe, and were probably only useful for systems where low level descriptions of the inputs and outputs were available, e.g. some process control systems. Our extensions to the techniques [Systems Designers Limited (1982b)] have increased the generality of the techniques, but it would still be difficult to describe certain classes of systems, e.g. database applications, within the notation. Our general assessment is that the techniques are suitable for a large proportion of embedded real-time systems, but certain classes of system may be awkward to specify using these techniques. Thus we might expect to see a different method for System and Abstract Functional Specification in an APSE developed for the production of Information Systems, for example.

ANNA is clearly limited in applicability, if only because of its inability to deal with tasks. This is a very severe problem, and we are unaware of a method or notation which satisfactorily addresses the problems of concurrency in real - time systems, although some relevant research is going on, e.g. that on Temporal Logic [Schwarz

and Melliar-Smith (1981)] and CCS [Milner (1980)]. The only
practicable approach at present seems to be use a language
such as ANNA to specify the sequential aspects of the system
and to rely on other techniques for specifying the parallel
aspects of the systems.

In   section 3.1 we identified SPECIAL-A [Roubine
(1982)] as a possible alternative to ANNA. SPECIAL-A may
prove to be more effective than ANNA in practice, but it
does not deal with concurrency, so we would still need a
separate method for handling concurrency if SPECIAL-A was
adopted.

Unfortunately there is a further problem
associated with using languages such as ANNA. Our experience
suggests that languages in the style of ANNA are difficult,
and therefore costly, formalisms to use. Although there are
benefits of having highly formal specifications we believe
that the cost of producing the formal specifications may
outweigh the benefits in all but the most critical systems.
We believe therefore that it will probably be more
appropriate to use informal notations in many application
areas, for some time to come. This situation could be
changed both by improvements in the intelligibility of the
specification languages, and by the production of good tool
support for the production and checking of system
representations expressed in these languages.

In summary we believe that a system based on
CORE, and the A-7 techniques would have a wide applicability
for real-time embedded systems. The langauge oriented design
representations pose a problem, but we hope that languages
such as ANNA or SPECIAL-A will become widely applicable when
they are more mature and a sufficiently high level of tool
support is available.

We believe that the the project management
techniques as described above are sufficiently general to be
applied to a large class of systems. The project management
techniques are unlikely to be a limiting factor in an APSE
based on the development techniques which we have
investigated.

4.4   Outline Development Plan

4.4.1   Introduction

This study has performed a first rapid iteration of a top-down APSE design process, and the data model and toolsets outlined in section 3.4 may be regarded as a draft design for an APSE. Further the study has shown that an APSE can profitably be based on a coherent set of methods, and shown that such an APSE could be built using the MAPSEs under development and existing tool technology.

The draft design has enabled us to show the technical feasibility of developing a coherent APSE with today's technology but it is not sufficiently detailed to be used for generating a detailed development plan. Nevertheless, given the list of support tools identified in section 3.4.2, we are in a position to outline a development plan. This plan identifies three steps in a large scale APSE development leading to:

1   a "Clerical Support APSE"

2   a "V&V and Management Support APSE" and

3   a "Transformation Support APSE".

These clearly correspond to the basic, aggregated and integrated toolsets which we introduced in section 3.4.2. From this view, an outline development plan for a cost-effective medium-scale APSE can be derived. We recommend that this plan for a medium-scale APSE be followed as we believe it will produce the best return for investment in terms of improving the productivity of the software industry, and improving the quality of the software that is poduced.

4.4.2   Further Design Iterations

The rapid iteration of the design process performed by this study with about a man-years effort, has to be followed by further iterations which will have to be far more thorough. The purpose of this design work would be to further consolidate the conceptual framework developed here and to generate a design for an APSE, in sufficient detail, and with sufficient confidence, to allow main-stream implementation work to begin.

It must be recognised that designing a full APSE is potentially a very major undertaking: for example, it could easily dwarf the Ada language design exercise. To some degree one would expect to "get what one pays for", probably with diminishing returns on larger investments.

In the same way, that the Ada design was "engineered", the APSE design should be organised with a study team, many reviews and considerable public scrutiny, under a fixed schedule, guaranteeing, if not the best possible design, at least a solid pragmatic result. As stated in the introduction, it is felt that many workers from various fields have a contribution to make. Therefore subsequent design iterations should be performed in as open a manner as possible, with many people contributing directly to the work and many more providing comments and review.

4.4.3   Steps in a large-scale APSE development

4.4.3.1   Introduction

The Stoneman document [Department of Defense (1980b)] advocates a bottom-up approach to APSE development which starts with the kernel and the minimal APSE (KAPSE and MAPSE), followed by the method-dependent advanced APSE tool development. In this study, we have concentrated solely on methods and tools which can be implemented on top of the MAPSE. As a consequence, we base our outline of an APSE development on the existence of a suitable MAPSE. We extend the Stoneman idea of bottom-up development into the APSE development by distinguishing three steps towards a full APSE. These steps are felt to be useful for several reasons:

1   They allow the the development effort to be based on major milestones, which is usually desirable for large scale developments.

2   They   allow for a more efficient development   as
    the   APSE resulting from one step can be used to
    aid   in   the   development of the APSE of the next
    step.

3   They   structure   the APSE development so that the
    sequence of steps reflects increasing

    - dependency among tools,
    - risk
    - difficulty of implementation
    - development costs
    - development duration
    - support sophistication
    - degree of support
    - difficulty   of   learning   to   use   the   APSE
      effectively.

4   They indicate a path for making the transition to
    the   full APSE which would be feasible for most
    organisations to follow.

4.4.3.2   MAPSE Availability

        The   steps   which we describe below are based on
the   assumption   that   a   suitable MAPSE is available at the
start of the implementation process.   The MAPSE must contain
the   basic   development support tools (compiler, editor,
debugger,...),   and most importantly, it must provide a data
base   management   system with a schema definition mechanism,
and   a data base traversal and navigation mechanism based on
a   query   language. It is assumed furthermore that the MAPSE
will   contain   various   tools   useful for the development of
language   processors,   e.g.   generators   of   lexical   and
syntactic   analysers,   compiler writing systems supporting
also   the   generation   of semantic analysers.   These "meta -
tools"   will be used in the production of the tools required
at each step.

4.4.3.3 First Step: "Clerical Support APSE"

The result of the first step will be an APSE providing tool support for entering, modifying and retrieving data in the data base in a way consistent with further APSE development. This step would develop:

1 Structural Editors - to assist in the generation of the data base representation for the various representations of the system and the project guide.

2 Syntactic Analysers - to check the syntax of the representations. These tools can be automatically generated from the formal descriptions of the representation languages by the above mentioned MAPSE-tools; these latter tools can also assist the production of the structural editors.

3 Report Generators - to produce dictionaries, cross-reference listings etc.

Assuming that the APSE methods and life cycle representations have been defined in sufficient detail in the preceding design iterations, the effort required to perform this step is estimated to be 10-20 man years over a period of two years. This, and all the subsequent estimates of effort, are inevitably very tentative. More precise estimates could only be produced by choosing a particular set of methods to be supported and performing some high-level APSE design work.

4.4.3.4 Second Step: "V&V and Management Support APSE"

The result of this step would be an APSE which, in addition to the clerical support of the first step APSE, provides some support for verification and for project management. The support tools are still human-driven rather than representation-driven. In particular, the production

and revision of the project guide need human skills.
Configuration control, however, is largely automated. This
step would develop:

1   Semantic Checkers - to assist in checking the
    completeness and consistency of the
    representations

2   A Browsing Tool - to allow browsing through all
    the documents held in the data base

3   A Graphical Editor - mainly for the requirements
    expression activity

4   The Configuration Control Tools (the nucleus,
    regeneration, coherency verification and
    archiving tools)

5   A PERT/Critical Path Analyser

6   A Project Guide Manipulation Tool

7   A Communication Path Definition Tool

8   Progress Monitoring and Indication Tools

9   A Graphical Display Tool - to display various
    management reports in graphical form

10 Various testing tools for Ada but based on
    existing techniques.

    Not including the testing tools, the effort for
this step is estimated to be 60-90 man years over a period
of three to four years.

4.4.3.5 Third Step: "Transformation Support APSE"
         The result of this last step would be a complete

APSE with active support for transforming representations
and for deriving and exploiting representation-based
management data. This step would develop:

1 Transformation Drivers - to assist in the
   generation of life cycle representations from
   higher-level ones

2 Modelling and Simulation Tools

3 Rapid Implementation Tools - to work on the
   principle of refinement by transformations

4 Rapid Prototyping Tools

5 A Symbolic Execution Tool

6 A Program Pover

7 Estimation and Statistical Analysis Tools

8 A Work Breakdown Tool

9 A Resource Allocation Aid

Of course, this list is by no means complete but
it can be taken as an indication of the kind of tools which
it would be beneficial to develop in this last step.

This step involves considerable research and the
effort to perform it will probably exceed 100 man years
spread over a period of five years or more.

4.4.4   An Outline APSE Development Plan

A large scale development proceeding in the
above-mentioned three steps would last a decade and involve
many people. Given the difficulty of justifying such a
development without substantial evidence of the efficacy of
the resultant product, and the scarcity of suitably skilled

manpower, it seems to be appropriate to aim at a more modest
APSE development which could be highly cost-effective. A
medium scale APSE development would still have to define the
crucially important conceptual framework for the full APSE.
Once a sound framework has been established the actual
development can proceed on an incremental basis.

    We therefore propose an outline plan
incorporating the initial design process and the development
of the most important and cost-effective tools from the
three steps:

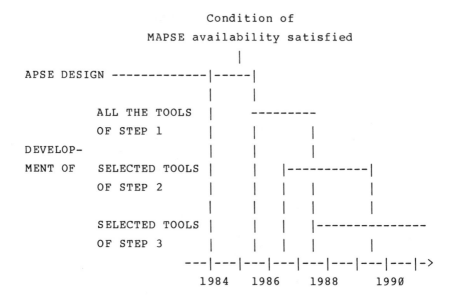

```
                      Condition of
                MAPSE availability satisfied

                          |
APSE DESIGN -------------|-----|
                          |     |
           ALL THE TOOLS  |   ---------
           OF STEP 1      |     |       |
DEVELOP-                  |     |       |
MENT OF   SELECTED TOOLS  |     |   |-----------|
          OF STEP 2       |     |   |   |       |
                          |     |   |   |       |
          SELECTED TOOLS  |     |   |   |---------------
          OF STEP 3       |     |   |   |       |
                 ---|---|---|---|---|---|---|---|->
                    1984    1986    1988    1990
```

    Given this situation where potentially enormous
effort could be invested but the rate of return is not quite
clear, some personal judgement is required. We would suggest
that a period of two years be allotted for a second design
iteration, with the widest possible participation. When a
MAPSE is available detailed design and implementation work
concerning the support tools should be started but the
investigation and design exercise should continue with the
intention of providing input for subsequent APSE evolution.
    The development of clerical support tools (step
1) should be started first so that they can be used for the

subsequent development of:

1   selected step 2 tools:
    - the Browsing Tool
    - Semantic Checkers for the high-level life-cycle
      representations
    - the Configuration Control Tools
    - the PERT/Critical Path Analyser

2   selected step 3 tools:
    - Transformation   Drivers   for   the   high-level
      life-cycle representations
    - Modelling/Simulation Tools
    - Estimation and Statistical Analysis Tools

Configuration control tools, PERT analyser and Modelling/Simulation Tools could be implemented by adopting existing tools.

The effort required for this medium-scale APSE development would be approximately:

APSE DESIGN	10-20
STEP1 TOOLS	10-20
SELECTED STEP2 TOOLS	30-60
SELECTED STEP3 TOOLS	30-60
	80-160 man years

During the development, the methods and tools already produced should themselves be used as much as possible. Furthermore, extensive use should be made of automatic generation techniques which generally enforce formalisation and lead to more readily understandable and modifiable systems.

4.5 Recommendations

These   recommendations are based on the existing
consensus that:

1 Current   software engineering technology needs to
   be improved.

2 It can be improved through the development and
   subsequent   use   of   programming   support
   environments in which coherent methods are
   supported by integrated tools.

Evidence of this consensus can be found in the
fact that several initiatives have been launched in an
attempt to improve the "state of the art" in Software
technology, e.g.:

1 the Ada programme of the US DoD, which led to the
   production of Stoneman [Department of Defense
   (1980b)] and several MAPSE developments

2 the proposed Extension of the Multi-Annual Data
   Processing Support Programme of the European
   Communities - more than one third of the support
   may go into the programming support environment
   area

3 the Software Technology Initiative of the US DoD
   [Department of Defense (1981)]

4 the European Strategic Programme for Research in
   Information Technology [ESPRIT (1982)]

5 the United Kingdoms Alvey programme.

The study on which this book is based has shown
that even a medium-scale APSE development necessitates a
considerable investment which is probably too large for most

individual Companies. Furthermore, the resources of highly qualified personnel necessary for this kind of development are probably too scarce within individual organisations. Only an initiative at at least national level would enable the potential benefits of an APSE development to be realised.

We therefore recommend that the cost-effective medium-scale APSE development outlined above should be supported with National or International funding. Within Europe a suitable support mechanism would be that of the Extended Multi-Annual Data Processing Support Programme planned for the period 1983-1987. After an initial period of top-down APSE design along the lines sketched in this book, the medium-scale APSE could be implemented using existing methods and technology. The resulting APSE would be a "pragmatic" APSE offering very substantial support however possibly not in all areas (e.g. not concurrent systems). This book has stressed an advanced microscopic view of system representations which requires a suitable data base management system. Alternatively substantial support could be achieved by a "simpler" APSE permitting only macroscopic views of the life cycle representations.

It is also worth pointing out that much of the development is of value to organisations producing systems in languages other than Ada. All the management methods and tools are applicable to non-Ada programming environments, and the methods for producing the Requirements Expression, System Specification and Abstract Functional Specification are generally applicable. Thus there is considerable benefit to be gained from developing the environment and tools described above even outside the Ada community.

The top-down design and incremental medium scale APSE development should be paralleled by bottom-up research which again should be supported at national or international level. This research should tackle particularly difficult aspects of software development (e.g. formal specification and verification of large systems). These projects should make use of the evolving APSE and contribute to the

development of a large-scale APSE. Again ESPRIT seems to be
the appropriate vehicle for this research programme within
Europe.

In order to demonstrate the cost-effectiveness
of the APSE being developed it would be valuable to apply
the methods to be supported by the APSE to a number of real
projects. One vehicle for this is the Application Area
Projects of the planned Multi-Annual Programme Extension,
which are intended to redevelop large industrial real-time
systems in Ada.

The biggest obstacles to the successful
introduction of an APSE as sketched in this book will be in
the areas of education and motivation of potential users. We
therefore feel that a top priority during the next three or
four years until the "Clerical Support APSE" becomes
available should be an industrial education programme
covering the major issues of software engineering and the
benefits of coherent methodologies. If various methodology -
related tools could be made available for use by this
programme, even in an ad-hoc fashion, then this could be of
considerable benefit.

It is anticipated that such an education
programme would create an awareness of the inadequacy of the
current technology, and a demand for a better technology.
With such a climate established the introduction of a
"Clerical Support APSE" should not present insurmountable
problems, and transition to a more complete APSE should
follow naturally.

References

Not all the references given below are cited in the text. The additional references are included because they give further information on methods and tools which we have referred to in the text.

M.W. Alford (1977), A requirements engineering methodology for real-time processing requirements, IEEE Trans. on Software Engineering. SE3, pp 60-69.

Atlantic Software (1970), SDM/70, Software Development Methodology.

Augusta Consortium (1981), Ada-based system methodology study report, available from the Department of Industry, London, UK.

H. Barringer and I. Mearns (1982), Axioms and Proof Rules for Ada Tasks, IEE Proceedings Vol. 129, Part E, No. 2.

BIGRE (1982), Actes des journees BIGRE 82, Systemes integres de production de logiciels, BIGRE No28-29.

B.W. Boehm (1976), Software Engineering, IEEE Transactions on Computers, C-25, No. 12.

B.W. Boehm (1981), Software Engineering Economics, Prentice-Hall, New York.

K.H. Britton and D.L. Parnas (1981), A-7E software module guide, NRL Memorandum Report 4702, Naval Research Laboratory, Washington D.C.

F. Brooks (1975), The Mythical Man-month - Essays in Software Engineering, Addison Wesley.

J.F. Caillet, J.F. Combes and M. Maisonneuve (1982), Le SGDL, un outil integre de production et de gestion de grands logiciels, in BIGRE No28-29, pp 155-171.

T.A. Cargill (1980), Management of the source text of a portable operating system, proc. of the Fourth Computer Software and Application Conference, pp 764-768.

P.M. Cashman and A.W. Holt (1980), A communication-oriented approach to structuring the software maintenance environment, Software Engineering Notes 5, no. 1, pp 4-17.

T.E. Cheatham (1981), An Overview of the Harvard Program Development System, in: [Hunke 81], pp 253-266.

T.E. Cheatham, G.H. Holloway and J.A. Townley (1981), Program refinement by transformation, in: Proc. 5th Int. Conf. on Software Engineering, IEEE, New York, pp 430-437.

P.S. Chen (1976), The entity-relationship model - toward a unified view of data, ACM Transactions on Database Systems 1, No1, pp 9-36.

CII - Honeywell - Bull (1982), ALPAGE (Atelier Logiciel pour la Programmation de Grande Envergure).

P.C. Clements (1981), Function specifications for the A-7E function driver module, NRL Memorandum Report 4658, Naval Research Laboratory Washington D.C.

E.F. Codd (1982), Relational Database: A practical foundation for productivity, CACM 25, No2, pp 109-117.

Computer 14, No4, (1981). Special issue on programming environments.

Computer 14, No6, (1981) Special issue on Ada.

M.L. Cook (1982), Software Metrics, An introduction and Annotated Bibliography, Software Engineering Notes 7, No. 2.

L.W. Cooprider (1978), The Representation of Families of Software Systems, PhD Thesis, Carnegie Mellon University.

E. Cristofor, T.A. Wendt and B.C. Wonsievicz (1980), Source Control + Tools = Stable Systems, Proc.of the

Fourth Computer Software and Applications Conference, pp 527-532.

E.B. Dalby (1980), Organisational Philosophies used in Software Development, Infotech State of the Art Review. Also in [Wasserman 81a].

Department of Defense (1980a), Ada Reference Manual.

Department of Defense (1980b), Stoneman, Requirements for Ada Programming Support Environments.

Department of Defense (1981), Candidate R&D Thrusts for the Software Technology Initiative.

Department of Defense (1982a), Ada Reference Manual.

Department of Defense (1982b), Software Development Methodologies and Ada (Methodman).

P. Deutsch and E.A. Taft (Eds) (1980), Requirements for an Experimental Programming Environment, Xerox Parc, CSL-80-10.

E.W. Dijkstra (1976), A discipline of programming, Prentice-Hall, Englewood Cliffs, NJ.

ESPRIT (1982), ESPRIT Technical Panel - Software Technology, Final Report, Document No. JEPE/TP3/WP/72.

J. Foisseau et al (1982), Recherches sur la conception de programmes assistee par ordinateur, Rapport Final No3607/DERI, CPAO/82/1, ONERA/CERT.

L.D. Fosdick and L.J. Osterweil (1976), Data Flow Analysis in Software Reliability, ACM Computing Surveys 8, 3.

S.J. Goldsack and V.A. Downes (1982), Programming Embedded Systems with Ada, Chapter 4, Prentice Hall.

J.P. Goldstein and D.G.Bobrow (1980), A Layered Approach to Software Design, Xerox Parc CSL-80-5.

D.I. Good (Ed) (1977), Constructing Verifiably reliable and secure communications processing systems, Tech. Rep. ICSCA-CMP-6, Univ. Texas at Austin.

J.V. Guttag (1977), Abstract data types and the development of data structures, CACM.6, pp 396-404.

J.V. Guttag and J.J. Horning (1978), The algebraic specification of abstract data types, Acta Informatica 10, pp 27-52.

M. Halstead (1977), Elements of Software Science, North
    Holland/Elsevier.

M. Hamilton and S. Zeldin (1976), Higher Order Software - a
    methodology for defining software, IEEE Trans. on
    Software Engineering. SE2, pp 9-32.

K.L. Heninger, J.W. Kallander, J.E. Shore and D.L. Parnas
    (1978), Software requirements for the A-7E
    aircraft, NRL Memorandum Report 3876, Naval
    Research Laboratory, Washington D.C.

W. Hesse (1981), Methoden und Werkzeuge zur Software -
    Entwicklung -- Ein Marsch durch die Technologie -
    Landschaft, Informatik Spektrum 4, pp 229-245.

S.D. Hester, D.L. Parnas and D.F. Utter (1981), Using
    Documentation as a Software Design Medium, The
    Bell System Technical Journal 60, no.8, pp
    1941-1977.

Honeywell Inc. and CII Honeywell Bull (1979), Rationale for
    the Design of the GREEN Programming Language.

W.E. Howden (1982), Contemporary Software Development
    Environments, CACM 25, no.5, pp 318-329.

K.E. Huff (1981), A Database model for effective
    configuration management in the programming
    environment, Proc. 5th Int. Conf. on Soft. Eng.,
    pp 54-61.

H. Hunke (Ed) (1981), Software Engineering Environments,
    North Holland, Amsterdam.

Intermetrics Inc. (1981), Ada Integrated Environment, Design
    Rationale: Technical Report IR-684.

M.A. Jackson (1975), Principles of program design, Academic
    Press.

J.P. Keller (1979), MIG 1/2 Effort Evaluation Methodology,
    TECSI Internal Report 01 32 00 TEC 002.

B. Krieg-Bruckner and D.C. Luckham (1980), ANNA: towards a
    language for annotating Ada programs, ACM Sigplan
    notices. 15,11, pp 128-138.

B. Krieg-Bruckner, D.C. Luckham, F.W. von Henke and O. Owe
    (1982), Draft Reference Manual for ANNA, a
    langauge for annotating Ada programs.

M.M. Lehman (1981), The Environment of Program Development, Maintenance Programming and Programming Support, in [Wasserman 81a].

M. Maisonneuve (1981), SGDL: un systeme de gestion et de developpement de logiciels bati sur la souch de PWB/Unix, in: Troisieme journee francophone sur l'informatique, Geneve.

M. Maisonneuve, J.P. Keller and M. Stocking (1981), SGDL. A Microprocessor Software Development and Management System based on PWB/Unix, in Proc. of the 4th International Conference on Software Engineering for Telecommunication Switching Systems, Coventry, pp 83-88.

R.W McGuffin, A.E. Elliston, B.R. Tranter and P.N. Westmacott (1979), CADES - software engineering in practice, in: Proc. 4th International Conf. on Software Engineering, IEEE, New York, pp 136-144.

E.D. Miller (Ed) (1979), Tutorial: Automated Tools for Software Engineering, IEEE, No. 7.

R. Milner (1980), A Calculus of Communicating Systems, Lecture Notes in Computer Science No. 92, G. Goos, J. Hartmanis (Eds), Springer Verlag.

D.S. Notkin and A.N. Habermann (1981), Software Development Environment Issues as related to Ada, in: [Wasserman 81a].

P.S. Newman (1982), Towards an integrated development environment, IBM Syst. Journal 21, No1, pp 81-107.

R.A. Parker, K.L. Heninger, D.L. Parnas and J.E. Shore (1980), Abstract interface specifications for the A-7E device interface module, NRL Memorandum Report 4385, Naval Research Laboratory, Washington D.C.

D.L. Parnas (1972), On the criteria to be used in decomposing systems into modules, CACM.15, pp 1053-1058.

D.L. Parnas (1976), On the design and development of program families, IEEE Trans. On Software Engineering.

SE2, pp 1-9.

H. Partsch and R. Steinbruggen (1981), A Comprehensive Survey of Program Transformation Systems, Technical University of Munich, Institut fur Informatik, Report TUM I8108.

J.M. Piquet (1981), Application pratique des travaux de Halstead 1977-1981, GLOBULE 3, Bulletin du Groupe de Travail "Genie Logiciel" de l'AFCET, pp 53-72.

J.C. Rault (1981), Les travaux francais de recherche et de developpement en matiere de Genie Logiciel, Globule, Bulletin du groupe de travail "Genie Logiciel" de l'AFCET, No3.

D.J. Reifer (1979), Tutorial: Software Management, IEEE, New York.

W.E. Riddle (1979), An event-based design methodology supported by DREAM, in: H.J. Schneider (Ed), Formal models and practical tools for information systems design, North Holland, Amsterdam, pp 93-108.

W.E. Riddle (1981), An assessment of DREAM, in: [Hunke 81], pp 191-221.

L. Robinson, K.N. Levitt, P.G. Neumann and A.K. Saxena (1976), A Formal Methodology for the design of Operating System Software, in Current Trends in Information Processing, vol. 1, R.T. Yeh (Ed), Prentice Hall.

M.J. Rochkind (1975), The source code control system, IEEE Trans. on Software Engineering, SE1, No4, pp 364-370.

D.T. Ross (1977), Structured Analysis (SA): a language for communicating ideas, IEEE Trans. on Software Engineering. SE3 pp 16-34.

O. Roubine (1982), SPECIAL-A: Definition Preliminaire, CII Honeywell Bull.

RSRE (undated), The handbook of the Pilot SDS, RSRE, Malvern, England.

RSRE (1982), Progress report on requirement specification working group, Seminar on large real-time software systems, RSRE, Malvern, England.

E. Schmidt (1982), U.C. Berkeley and Xerox PARC, private
        communications.

D.J. Schultz (1979), A case study in system integration
        using the build approach, Proc. ACM Nat. Conf.,
        New York, pp 143-151.

R.L. Schwarz and M.P. Melliar - Smith (1981), Temporal Logic
        Specification of Distributed Systems, Proc. 2nd
        Int. Conf.on Distributed Systems, IEEE No.
        81CH1591-7.

B.A. Silverberg (1981), An overview of the SRI Hierarchical
        Development Methodology, in [Wasserman 81a],
        211-227.

Software Sciences Limited, SPL International, Systems
        Designers Limited and International Computers
        Limited (1981), UK Ada Study: final technical
        report. Vols 1-7. Available from the Librarian,
        Division of Numerical Analysis and Computer
        Science, NPL, Teddington, Middlesex, England.

N.V. Stenning, T. Froggatt, R. Gilbert and E. Thomas (1981),
        The Ada Environment: A Perspective, Computer 14,
        No. 6, pp 26-36.

Systems Designers Limited (1978), CORE   -   Controlled
        Requirements Expression, Seminar Notes.

Systems Designers Limited and Software Sciences Limited
        (1979), Ada Support System Study, Phase 3 Report.

Systems Designers Limited (1980), Requirements Specification
        techniques study for UK MoD - survey reports.

Systems Designers Limited (1982a), Burglar Alarm System -
        Requirements Expression, Document Reference
        C1640/BAS/1.

Systems Designers Limited (1982b), Burglar Alarm System -
        System Specification, Document Reference
        C1640/BAS/2.

Systems Designers Limited (1982c), Burglar Alarm System -
        Abstract Functional Specification, Document
        Reference C1640/BAS/6.

Systems Designers Limited (1982d), Burglar Alarm System -

Module   Specification,   Document   Reference
C1640/BAS/4.

Systems Designers Limited (1982e), Burglar Alarm System -
Module   Decomposition,   Document   Reference
C1640/BAS/3.

Systems Designers Limited (1982f), Burglar Alarm System -
Module Code, Document Reference C1640/BAS/5.

Systems Designers Limited (1982g), Burglar Alarm System -
Checks on Transformations, Document Reference
C1640/BAS/7.

Systems Designers Limited (1982h), Burglar Alarm System -
Processing   a   Change,   Document   Reference
C1640/BAS/8.

Systems Designers Limited and TECSI-Software (1982),
Life-Cycle Support in the Ada Environment, First
Interim Report to the CEC.

Systems Designers Limited (1983),   PERSPECTIVE: An
Introduction and Overview.

D. Teichrow and A. Hershey (1977), PSL/PSA: a computer-aided
technique   for   structured   documentation   and
analysis of information processing systems, IEEE
Trans. on Software Engineering. SE3, pp 41-48.

W.F.Tichy (1980), Software Development Control Based on
System Structure Description, PhD Thesis, CMU
Comp. Sci. Dept., CMU-CS-80-120.

W.F. Tichy (1982), Adabase: A Data Base for Ada Programs,
AdaTEC '82 Conference on Ada,.

C.E Walston and C.P. Felix (1977), A method of programming
measurement and estimation, IBM Syst. Journal 16
No.1, pp 54-73.

A.I. Wasserman (1980), Toward integrated software
development environments, Scientia 115, pp
663-684.

A.I. Wasserman (Ed) (1981a) Tutorial: Software Development
Environments, IEEE, New York.

A.I. Wasserman (1981b), The user software engineering
methodology: an overview, Tech. Rept. No.56,
Laboratory of Medical Information Science,

University of California, San Francisco.

A.I. Wasserman (1981c), Software tools in the User Software Engineering environment, in [Wasserman 81a], pp 181-194.

A.I. Wasserman and G. Gutz (1982), The future of programming.

A.I. Wasserman, J.S. Yeh, D.S. Keller (1981), The Module Control System, Technical Report No.51, Laboratory of Medical Information Science, University of California, San Francisco. (Submitted for publication)

P. Zave (1982), An Operational Approach to Requirements Expression for Embedded Systems, IEEE Trans. on Software Engineering, SE8, No3, pp250-269.

Annex 1

Use of the methods

1   INTRODUCTION

1.1   Scope of the Annex

In the study from which this book is derived we made experimental use of the development methods described in section 3.1. We did this in order to gain some evidence as to the efficacy of the individual methods, in particular, and of coherent methodologies in general. This experiment is documented at considerable length in [Systems Designers Limited (1982a-h)].

The main part of the experiment was concerned with making a series of transformations from a Requirements Expression for a system to the production of Module Code. Two subsidiary experiments investigated in detail the verification of the Module Code against the Requirement, via the intermediate representations, and investigated the ease with which changes in the Requirement could be incorporated into the other representations. This form of experiment was chosen in order that all the major aspects of a complete software development cycle could be investigated.

The first six of these documents [Systems Designers Limited (1982a-f)] contain representations for all, or a major part of, the system with which we experimented. The first document contains the Requirements Expression, produced in the notation of CORE. The second contains the System Specification produced in the A-7 notation, and so on. In addition each of these six documents contains a definition of the notation used, and an assessment of the efficacy of the method used.

The seventh document contains a record of the

checks needed to show that the Module Code correctly
implements the Requirements Expression. The eighth document
contains a record of the changes in the representations
which were made as a consequence of making a change in the
system requirements.

This annex contains excerpts from the record of
this experiment [Systems Designers Limited (1982a-h)]. The
aim of the annex is to give the reader an idea of the style
and characteristics of the methods, and of some of the major
benefits and drawbacks of the methods, without deluging him
with detail. As a consequence, however, this annex does not
contain enough information to allow the reader to apply the
methods described, nor does it show all the benefits and
drawbacks of the methods.

The excerpts which follow were chosen to make
clear the characteristics of the methods. They do not give a
complete picture of the system, but they do give a complete
history of the development of one part of the system, so it
is possible to see how the individual methods fit together.
For each method only enough of the notation is described to
allow the excerpt to be understood.

1.2   The Subject of the Experiment

The system used in the experiment was a
computerised monitor for a set of burglar alarms, known as
the Burglar Alarm System or BAS. This system was chosen
primarily because it was small enough to be tackled during
the study, but nonetheless sufficiently complex that it
presented some genuine problems of analysis and design.
Additionally one of the contributors had previously built
such a system so he was able to act in the role of customer
for the system, and we could use his experience of the
original development as a control against which to judge the
performance of the experiment.

The requirements for the BAS are described in
more detail in section 2 of this annex, but it is helpful to
give an informal overview of the system here, particularly
in order to introduce some terminology. The BAS is intended

to monitor the state of up to 5000 Burglar Alarms, and to notify an Operator if undesirable events (such as a break-in) are reported by one or more of the Burglar Alarms. The BAS is a centralised system, connected to the Burglar Alarms via leased lines.

Each "customer" of the BAS is known as a Subscriber, and communication between the BAS and the Subscriber is via an individual known as the Subscriber Contact. The BAS is tended by an Operator and a Supervisor. If the BAS reports an undesirable event then the Operator (or Supervisor) must notify the Subscriber Contact of this occurrence. The Subscriber Contact is responsible for any further action including contacting the Police.

The BAS is intended to replace existing equipment (banks of lights), but the existing equipment will remain in place to act as a back-up should the BAS fail.

2   REQUIREMENTS EXPRESSION

2.1   Scope of the Excerpt

A complete Requirements Expression (RE) produced using the CORE method [Systems Designers Limited (1978)] would contain a definition of a viewpoint hierarchy for the system, an operational requirement, a system requirement, definitions of the structure of the data objects, and some annexes recording decisions concerning the scope of the requirement, performance parameters etc. The operational requirement is concerned with the system and the environment in which it works. The system requirement is only concerned with the system which we intend to develop. The viewpoint hierarchy defines the set of views of all the people and organisations which interact with the system, and may include the system itself.

This excerpt contains a viewpoint hierarchy for the BAS and the system requirement. Where necessary we have included performance parameters and the important decisons in the text. Normally this information would be contained in annexes to the RE.

2.2   The Viewpoint Hierarchy

2.2.1   Overview and Notation

The viewpoint hierarchy shows the relationships between the different viewpoints of the system held by people and organisations which interact with the system. The purpose of having the viewpoint hierarchy is to guide the information gathering process, and to provide a framework for checking the consistency of the information given to the requirements analyst by these people and organisations.

The viewpoint hierarchy for the BAS is shown in Figure 1. The viewpoint hierarchy shows all the viewpoints and mechanisms pertinent to the use of the BAS, and the viewpoint of the development team. The notation means that the views on one level of the diagram are subviews of the parent view on the higher level. Thus the supervisor (of the BAS) has a view of the BAS which is a subset of that of the central station (where the BAS resides). The viewpoints

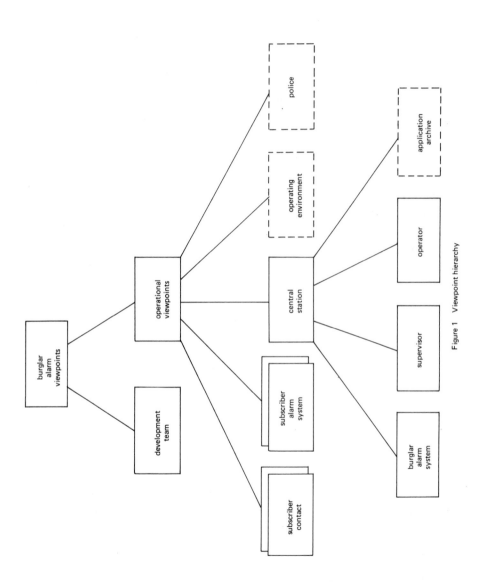

Figure 1 Viewpoint hierarchy

shown dotted are indirect viewpoints, that is they influence the behaviour of the system but are not directly involved in its use. Thus, for example, the Police are an influence on the system, but they are represented by an indirect viewpoint as they do not interact with the system.

2.2.2 Important Viewpoints

The viewpoint hierarchy in Figure 1 shows the operational and development views of the system. We will only be concerned with the operational views.

A Subscriber is someone whose premises are monitored with the assistance of the BAS. Each Subscriber is represented by a Subscriber Alarm System and by a Subscriber Contact who is the person to be contacted in the event of an alarm being raised.

Many Subscribers will be supported simulataneously. The "Maximum Number of Subscribers" is a parameter to the requirement which is expected to be in the range 3000 to 5000. The Subscriber responsibilities would normally be described in the Operational Requirement part of the RE (which is omitted from this annex).

The Operating Environment is a representation of the disturbing influences on the Subscriber Alarm Systems. The Police are an external receiver of outputs (alarm signals). The activities of the operating environment are not defined in this annex.

The BAS will not interact directly with the Police. It can, via the Subscriber Contact, cause interactions with the Police.

The Application Archive exists at the Central Station where the BAS itself resides. The Archive provides a record of all the key information which flows in and out of the Central Station. The activities of those responsible for the Application Archive are not defined in this annex.

The Supervisor and the Operator work at the Central Station and currently monitor the existing hardware. They will become responsible for the BAS when it takes over the monitoring of the Subscribers' Alarm Systems.

The Supervisors and Operators responsibilities would be described in more detail in the Operational Requirement in a full RE.

2.3 The System Requirement
2.3.1 Overview and Notation

The System Requirement is the most important part of the RE since it forms the main input to the production of the System Specification. The description presented here is very brief, but is probably of the appropriate length for a system of this size.

The BAS is described with reference to Figure 2. There are two eventualities which could arise which the customer for the system says are outside the scope of the requirement. First it is statistically possible that so many Subscriber Alarm Systems may simultaneously require attention that the BAS becomes overloaded. Second it is possible that a fault in the Subscriber Alarm Systems could cause rapid cycling of the reported alarm states. This could also overload the BAS. No allowance is made for these eventualities which will have to be detected by manual monitoring of the BAS.

In Figure 2 the rectangular boxes represent actions. These actions form a hierarchy, with certain predefined relationships. Actions shown vertically above one another can occur simultaneously. Actions to the left of the diagram must happen before those to the right. Subactions must occur within the operation of their parent actions. An asterisk at the top left hand corner of the rectangle indicates that the action is repetitive. A small circle in the top left hand corner of the rectangle indicates that the action is an alternate with those actions immediately above or below which are also marked with circles.

The lines in Figure 2 represent data flows. The names of the data flows are given beside the lines, and the name of the viewpoint in which the data structure is defined

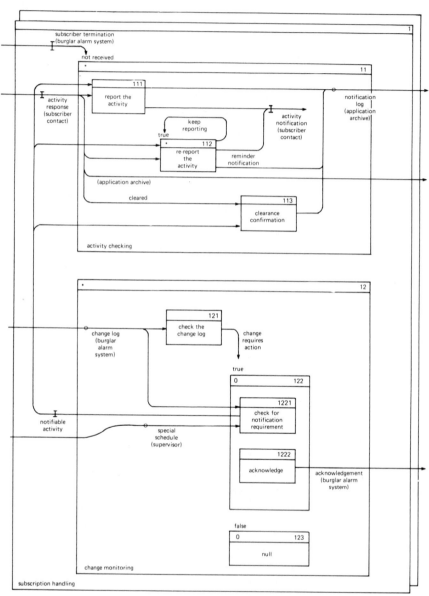

Figure 2   System operation (operator)

is given in parentheses. The direction of the data flows is made clear by the arrows. Lines carrying a small "I" are called "critical" data flows. This means that the consumer of the data flow must respond to each new data value. Data flows marked by a small circle are "non-critical", and represent looser synchronisation between the actions. Data flows into the top of an action are controls on that action, and any actions directly below it. On repetitive actions the control is the condition for repetition to continue, and on alternates it is the data on which the choice of alternate is made.

2.3.2 System Behaviour

The BAS interfaces a Supervisor and an Operator to a number of Subscriber Alarm Systems. The BAS is required to monitor each Subscriber's Current Reported State, which is the output from his Burglar Alarm. It will be adequate to sample this state so long as the sampling rate does not fall below once every 2.5 seconds.

The BAS must be capable of performing the functions described below for each Subscriber regardless of the Current Reported State of the other Subscribers' Alarm Systems.

The schedules define the legal opening times for each Subscriber's premises. The BAS must accept a Subscriber's Initial Schedule from the Supervisor, store it, and produce a record of the schedule for the Supervisor. The BAS should not perform any other functions pertaining to that particular Subscriber until it has an initial schedule for that Subscriber. Once the initial schedule has been received by the BAS it should support Alarm State Monitoring for that Subscriber, as described below, until the Supervisor inputs a Termination Message for that Subscriber. The BAS should allow the Supervisor to update the stored schedule by supplying a Subscriber's New Normal Schedule, after the initial schedule has been entered, and before a termination message has been entered for that subscriber.

The BAS must also accept Acknowledgements from

the Supervisor or Operator for the purposes described below.

The remaining inputs which the BAS receives are the Current Reported States from the Subscribers' Burglar Alarm Systems. This information is used by the BAS to perform the actions Opening Checks and Change Detection shown in Figure 2.

Opening Checks are performed at least once every hour, but preferably once every five minutes, for all current Subscribers (i.e. Subscribers for whom an initial schedule has been received, but no termination message has been received). The Current Reported State is compared with the Current Stored Schedule to determine whether or not the Subscriber's premises are open outside their scheduled hours (loosely referred to as "open late"). If the premises are open late then Change Reporting occurs, as described below.

Change Detection samples the Current Reported State at least once every 2.5 seconds. The BAS compares this sampled state with a record of the history of line states to determine whether or not a change has occurred since the last sample. If a change has occurred then the details are passed to Change Reporting.

Change Reporting reports the change or open late condition to the Central Station staff and records it on the Change Log in the Application Archive. Expected changes - i.e. the premises opening or closing between the times stated in the Stored Schedule - are only reported once. All other changes are reported at a high rate until the Supervisor or Operator enters an Acknowledgement, and thereafter at a low rate until the conditon clears.

A high rate of reminders is once every one to five minutes. A low rate is once every fifteen minutes to one hour.

2.4 Commentary

The RE produced using CORE is sufficiently similar to a conventional prose specification to be acceptable and accessible to the customer for a system. The CORE analyses, together with the well-defined notation, give the analyst the opportunity of producing a much more precise, consistent and complete RE than is possible with conventional prose specifications.

3   SYSTEM SPECIFICATION

3.1   Overview and Notation

     As explained in section 3.1.3 the SS was produced using the A-7 method [Heninger et al (1978), Systems Designers Limited (1982b)] and it contains definitions of the functions to be performed by the system. It also defines the Logical Output Data Items (LODI) the Real World Available Information (RWAI), the Auxiliary Data Items (ADI) and some information recording the mappings between these logical objects and the physical input/output devices. In this excerpt we consider only one function and the data items which are input to, or output from, that function.

     The data items are defined in a syntactic notation in the style of BNF. The values of terminal symbols in the syntax are left for definition during the system design. The types of data item are denoted by the following convention, viz:

     /This_is_an_input/
     //This_is_an_output//
     ///This_is_an_Auxiliary_Data_Item///

The function transfer characteristic is defined in a tabular form, which should be self explanatory. For each function an initiation and termination condition is specified. In the example, the initiation condition is of the form:

     @T(PRESENT (/Some_Input/))

This means that the function executes once the data item /Some_Input/ is present, i.e. has been input to the BAS.

     For the purposes of this excerpt it is necessary to know that the Supervisor and Operator interact with the BAS through a VDU and the Application Archive is produced on a lineprinter.

3.2   RWAI

Input Item: Subscribers Initial Schedule Details

Acronym: /Init_Sched_Details/

Source: Supervisor

Description:

/Init_Sched_Details/ gives the initial opening schedule for a new subscriber. Implicitly the presentation of this information causes the monitoring and change reporting functions to be initiated for the new subscriber (assuming that the data is valid). The data consists of a subscriber identifier (an integer in the range 1...5000) followed by a sequence of names of days together with their associated opening and closing times.

Data Representation:

/Init_Sched_Details/ ::= <Subscriber_Identifier>
                        <Openings_List>
                        Is_Init_Schedule

<Subscriber_Identifier> ::= Integer

<Openings_List> ::= null | <Days_Opening> <Openings_List>

<Days_Opening> ::= <Name_of_Day> Open_Time
                   <Lunch_Break> Close_Time

<Name_of_Day> ::= Mon | Tues | Weds | Thur | Fri | Sat | Sun

<Lunch_Break> ::= null | Close_Time Open_Time

Comment:

The values and formats of the terminal symbols,

e.g. Close_Time, must be defined by the Module Specification at the latest.

3.3 LODI

Output Item: Current Schedule

Acronym: //Curr_Sched//

Destinations: Supervisor, Application Archive

Description:

The Current Schedule is the most recently entered opening schedule for each subscriber. This will initially be /Init_Sched_Details/, and subsequently be the value of the new schedules entered into the BAS.

Data Representation:

//Curr_Sched// ::= <Subscriber_Identifier>
                   <Openings_List>
                   Is_Current_Schedule Date_Time

<Openings_List> is defined in section 3.2.

Comments:

The formats of //Curr_Sched// as displayed to the Supervisor and stored in the Application Archive need not be the same, although they must contain the same information. The display to the Supervisor may be presented concurrently with the input of the associated data item (e.g. /Init_Sched_Details/).

3.4 ADI

Auxiliary Item: Subscribers Active

Acronym: ///Subs_Active///

Description:

          ///Subs_Active/// indicates which subscribers
have had an initial schedule accepted and have not yet been
terminated.

Data Representation:

///Subs_Active/// ::= Set_of_Bool

Comment:

          ///Subs_Active///   indexed   on   <Subscriber_
Identifier> (see section 3.2) gives   the   activity state for
that subscriber.

    3.5 Function

Demand Function Name: Initiate Subscriber

Input Items: /Init_Sched_Details/, ///Subs_Active///

Output Items: //Curr_Sched//, ///Subs_Active///

Initiation Condition: @T (PRESENT (/Init_Sched_Details/))

Termination Condition:

          This is a demand function so the termination
condition does not need to be specified.

Function:

          We introduce two mnemonics for parts of the
input data item /Init_Sched_Details/ to simplify the
function description. Using the Ada "." convention for
selecting elements from structures these are:

/Subs_Id/ = /Init_Sched_Details/.<Subscriber_Identifier>

/Openings/ = /Init_Sched_Details/.<Openings_List>

Similarly for the ADI:

///Active/// = ///Subs_Active///(/Subs_Id/)

```
----------------------------------------------------------------
|          Input            |              Output               |
|---------------------------|-----------------------------------|
| ///Active/// | /Openings/ | ///Active/// | //Curr_Sched//     |
|---------------------------|-----------------------------------|
|    TRUE      |     -      |    TRUE      | unchanged          |
|---------------------------|-----------------------------------|
|    FALSE     |   Valid    |    TRUE      | (/Subs_Id/,        |
|              |            |              |  /Openings/,       |
|              |            |              |  Date_Time)        |
|---------------------------|-----------------------------------|
|    FALSE     |  Invalid   |    FALSE     | unchanged          |
----------------------------------------------------------------
```

Comments:
        We do not specify how invalid inputs should be
handled in terms of error messages to the Supervisor. The
nature of valid and invalid schedules, and lower level data
invalidities, such as illegal times, should be defined by
the Module Specification stage.

    3.6 Commentary
        The A-7 notation allows us to give quite precise
definitions of the data structures and of the transfer
characteristics of the functions. It also enables us to mix
in prose comments where prose is more perspicuous than
formal descriptions. This, we believe, makes the A-7
techniques easy to use and it means that the representations
produced are quite precise, yet much easier to understand
than if they had been produced entirely in a formal
notation.
        In the example shown above we have deferred a
number of decisions, e.g. the definition of what constitutes

a valid opening schedule, and how to handle invalid schedules to a later stage. In retrospect this was a mistake and it would be desirable to make these decisions at this stage. In practice it could be awkward to incorporate this information in the SS as the notation is not particularly well-suited to specifying man/machine dialogues.

4   ABSTRACT FUNCTIONAL SPECIFICATION

4.1   Overview and Notation

The AFS consists of the definition of data items and functions in much the same style as the SS. The only significant difference is that it is necessary to represent hierarchies of functions in the AFS. This is done by having "composite functions" which are composed out of "basic functions". The basic functions are defined by means of a transfer function in the same way as the functions in the SS. The form of the composite functions is illustrated below.

The excerpt is the schedule checking subfunction from the function which reads, checks and installs new and initial functions (called Initiate_or_Update in the AFS). Only the schedule checking composite function is shown below. The basic function which is used (Check_Day_Sched) checks the validity of a schedule for one day and returns a boolean which is TRUE if the schedule is valid and FALSE otherwise. The meaning of the data items which are used are assumed to be clear from their names.

Since we have "common use" functions in the AFS we have to show the basic functions with formal parameters, and show the formal to actual parameter mappings when we use the basic functions. We also use object attributes in much the same way as attributes in Ada, for example, to control function execution.

4.2   Composite Function

Demand Function: Check_Sched

Input: /Sched/

Output: //Sched_OK//

Locals: ///OK_so_far/// initialised to TRUE
        ///Last_Sched/// initialised to /Sched/'First

Function:

Invokes Check_Day_Sched, iterating through the daily schedules in /Sched/.

Parameter Bindings:

Initial Iteration

Formal	/Day_Sched/	//Day_Sched_OK//	//Sched_Out//
Actual	/Sched/'First	///OK_so_far///	///Last_Sched///

Subsequent Iterations

Formal	/Day_Sched/	//Day_Sched_OK//	//Sched_Out//
Actual	/Sched/'Next	///OK_so_far///	///Last_Sched///

Initiation: On entering Check_Sched

Termination: @T(///Last_Sched/// = /Sched/'Last
OR NOT ///OK_so_far///)

Output Value:

//Sched_OK// has the value of ///OK_so_far/// on exit from Check_Sched.

4.3 Commentary

It should be clear from the above excerpt that the formalism for expressing function composition is rather clumsy. Essentially the problem is that we wish to show the functional composition, which is a control flow concept, within a functional notation. This aspect of the notation would have to be improved before the method could be widely used.

5 MODULE SPECIFICATION AND CODE

5.1 Overview and Notation

In our interpretation of the Life Cycle Model we had three programming language oriented representations: the Module Specification, the Module Design and the Module Code. In our experiment we found that there was sufficient information in the MS to allow us to proceed directly to the MC without producing the MD. In this excerpt we reproduce the corresponding parts of the MS and MD, side by side, in order to make clear the relationships between these two representations.

We assume that it is unnecessary to describe the "notation" of Ada, however we do remind the reader that our experiment used the 1980 version of the language [Department of Defense (1980a)]. We present a summary of the features of ANNA [Krieg-Bruckner and Luckham (1980)] sufficient to allow the reader to understand the excerpt.

All statements in ANNA are represented as comments in an Ada compilation unit. ANNA statements are distinguished from other comments by use of a special comment sysmbol "--|".

ANNA is an extended form of the predicate calculus couched in a syntactic form similar to Ada. The universal quantifier is represented as "forall" and the existential quantifier as "exists". The concept of array updates which is foreign to the predicate calculus is included in ANNA by the introduction of a special "attribute" of each array type, as illustrated below:

```
type ARRAY_TYPE is array (1...MAX) ELEMENT_TYPE;


INSTANCE_OF_ARRAY: ARRAY_TYPE;


--| ARRAY_TYPE'UPDATE(INSTANCE_OF_ARRAY,
--|                   INDEX =>
--|                   INSTANCE_OF_ELEMENT_TYPE
--|                   )
```

The last four lines are an ANNA statement representing the assignment of INSTANCE_OF_ELEMENT_TYPE to the INDEXth element of INSTANCE_OF_ARRAY.

Statements in ANNA include tautologies which relate the inputs to a procedure to the output from the procedure. The statment takes the form of:

where boolean_expression.

The boolean expression must evaluate to TRUE. In ANNA annotations the input and output values to a procedure are denoted by the prefixes "in" and "out" respectively.

In our excerpt we consider the specification and implementation of a task. This shows the artifice which we used to handle tasks in ANNA. A number of packages are used by the task in question. We do not include those packages here and it is hoped that the reader will be able to interpret the meaning of the data types, data items and functions in those packages from their names. In any event the excerpt should give the reader an idea of the style and nature of an ANNA specification.

5.2   Specification and Code

The excerpt is the task which reads, checks and stores new and initial schedules, and makes a record of the schedules in the Application Archive (on the printer).

```
with SUBSCRIBER_SCHEDULES; use SUBSCRIBER_SCHEDULES;
-- repository for the schedules
with CLOCK; use CLOCK;
with VDU_INTERFACE; use VDU_INTERFACE;
--   this package delivers only syntactically correct REPORTs
--   containing schedules to the task
with PRINTER_INTERFACE; use PRINTER_INTERFACE;
with SCHEDULES_AND_REPORTS; use SCHEDULES_AND_REPORTS;
-- defines the types used in this package


package INITIATION_AND_UPDATE is


task INIT_AND_UPD;


-- This  task  checks  the semantics  of  a  new  or initial
-- schedule  entered  into  the  system  and  places a valid
-- schedule  into  the permanent record of schedules held by
-- the package SUBSCRIBER_SCHEDULES.


-- We  introduce a procedure which represents one activation
-- of  the  task,  and  present an ANNA specification of the
-- behaviour  of  that  procedure.  Some of the data objects
-- referred  to  are  variables  introduced to represent the
-- states  of other packages. In a full MS all these objects
-- would be properly defined.


--| procedure ONE_INIT_OR_UPD (R: in REPORT,
--|                               V, L: out REPORT);


-- R  is the input from the VDU containing the schedule etc.
-- and  V  and  L  are the output to the VDU and Lineprinter
-- respectively.


-- R is obtained by calling the entry GET_SCHEDULE in VDU_IF
-- and  V and L are output by calling the entries PUT_REPORT
-- in VDU_IF and PRINTER_IF respectively.  The date and time
-- are  obtained  by  calls  on  GET_DATE   and   GET_TIME
-- respectively in CLOCK.
```

```
package body INITIATION_AND_UPDATE is

task body INIT_AND_UPD is

   INR, OUTR: REPORT;
   DATE: DATE;
   TIME: TIME;
   SUBS_EXISTS: BOOLEAN;
   DAYS_OK: BOOLEAN;
```

```
--| where out L = out V
--| and
--| ((not (in R.SUBS_ID > 0
--|        and not in R.SUBS_ID > MAX_SUBS
--|        )
--|   and out V = (SCHED_PLUS,
--|                in R.SUBS_ID,
--|                in DATE_TIME,
--|                in R.SCHED,
--|                INVALID_SUBS_ID
--|                )
--|  )
--| or
--| (in R.SUBS_ID > 0
--|  and not in R.SUBS_ID > MAX_SUBS
--|  and ( (in SUBS_ACTIVE(in R.SUBS_ID)
--|         and in R.TYPE = INIT_SCHED
--|         and out V = (SCHED_PLUS,
--|                      in R.SUBS_ID,
--|                      in DATE_TIME,
--|                      in R.SCHED,
--|                      SUBS_ALREADY_ACTIVE
--|                      )
--|        )
--|       or
--|       (not in SUBS_ACTIVE(in R.SUBS_ID)
--|        and in R.TYPE = INIT_SCHED
--|        and out V = (SCHED_PLUS,
--|                     in R.SUBS_ID,
--|                     in DATE_TIME,
--|                     in R.SCHED,
--|                     SUBS_NOT_ACTIVE
--|                     )
--|        )
```

```
begin
  loop
    VDU_IF.GET_SCHEDULE(INR);
    CLOCK.GET_TIME(TIME);
    CLOCK.GET_DATE(DATE);
    DAYS_OK := TRUE;
    if INR.SUBS_ID > MAX_SUBS
       or INR.SUBS_ID < 1
      then
        OUTR := (SCHED_PLUS,
                 INR.SUBS_ID,
                 (DATE,TIME),
                 INR.SCHED,
                 INVALID_SUBS_ID
                );
      else
        SUBS_SCHEDULES.SUBS_EXISTS(INR.SUBS_ID,SUBS_EXISTS);
        if SUBS_EXISTS and INR.REPT_TYPE = INIT_SCHED
          then
            OUTR := (SCHED_PLUS,
                     INR.SUBS_ID,
                     (DATE,TIME),
                     INR.SCHED,
                     SUBS_ALREADY_ACTIVE
                    )
          else if not SUBS_EXISTS
                  and INR.REPT_TYPE = NEW_SCHED
              then
                OUTR := (SCHED_PLUS,
                         INR.SUBS_ID,
                         (DATE,TIME),
                         INR.SCHED,
                         SUBS_NOT_ACTIVE
                        );
```

```
--|              or
--|              ( (     (in SUBS_ACTIVE(in R.SUBS_ID)
--|                    and in R.TYPE = NEW_SCHED
--|                    )
--|                or (not in SUBS_ACTIVE(in R.SUBS_ID)
--|                    and in R.TYPE = INIT_SCHED
--|                    )
--|                )
--|              and ( (forall D: DAY =>
--|                     VALID(in R.SCHED(D))
--|                     and out V = (SCHED_PLUS,
--|                                  in SUBS_ID,
--|                                  in DATE_TIME,
--|                                  in R.SCHED,
--|                                  IS_NEW_SCHEDULE
--|                                  )
--|                     and out SCHEDS = SCHEDS'UPDATE
--|                                     (in SCHEDS,
--|                                      in R.SUBS_ID =>
--|                                      in R.SCHED
--|                                      )
--|                     and out SUBS_ACTIVE = SUBS_RECORD'UPDATE
--|                                     (in SUBS_ACTIVE,
--|                                      in R.SUBS_ID =>
--|                                      TRUE
--|                                      )
--|                     )
--|                 or (exists D: DAY =>
--|                     not VALID(in R.SCHED(D))
--|                     and out V = (SCHED_PLUS,
--|                                  in R.SUBS_ID,
--|                                  in DATE_TIME,
--|                                  in R.SCHED,
--|                                  INVALID_SCHEDULE
--|                                  )
--|             ))))));
```

```
        else
          for DAY in DAY'RANGE loop
            if DAYS_OK
              then
                SUBS_SCHEDULES.PUT_DAY_SCHEDULE
                              (INR.SUBS_ID,
                               INR.SCHED(DAY),
                               DAYS_OK,
                               DAY = SUN
                              );
              else
                 exit
            end if;
          end loop;
          if DAYS_OK
            then
              OUTR := (SCHED_PLUS,
                       INR.SUBS_ID,
                       (DATE,TIME),
                       INR.SCHED,
                       IS_NEW_SCHEDULE
                      );
            else
              OUTR := (SCHED_PLUS,
                       INR.SUBS_ID,
                       (DATE,TIME),
                       INR.SCHED,
                       INVALID_SCHEDULE
                      );
          end if;
        end if;
      end if;
      VDU_IF.PUT_REPORT(OUTR);
      PRINTER_IF.PUT_REPORT(OUTR);
    end loop;
  end INIT_AND_UPD;
end INITIATION_AND_UPDATE;
```

5.3   Commentary

One of the most striking aspects of this excerpt is the similarity in the amount of detail in the code and in the ANNA specification. This excerpt is quite typical of the rest of the System Specification, in this respect. As pointed out in section 3.1.5 this may be attributable to our inexperience with ANNA, the nature of the problem, or the nature of ANNA itself. Since ANNA was designed for annotation we believe that the nature of ANNA was the main factor causing the high level of detail in the specification.

Ideally, in a top-down development process, we should be able to produce specifications which are much more succinct and much more abstract than than the implementation itself. If this is not possible then much of the point of having the specification is lost, and it might be more cost-effective for the specifier to produce the implementation rather than a specification. However if we wished to verify the properties of a program then the level of detail present in the ANNA specification would be much more appropriate.

Our artifice for specifying the behaviour of the task is, we believe, reasonably satisfactory in this example, as the semantics of the program have been minimally distorted. For tasks which operated as "object managers" modelling the task as a set of procedures where one procedure corresponded to one entry was also quite satisfactory. For more complex tasks, e.g. those which are both active, and providers of services, our technique is much less satisfactory.

Clearly a better approach to the specification of the properties of concurrent systems is needed.

6   SUBSIDIARY EXPERIMENTS

6.1   Checks on Transformations

6.1.1   Introduction

The   checks on the transformations are of a very similar   form between each two levels of representation. We therefore illustrate the verification process as recorded in [Systems   Designers   Limited (1982g)] by an excerpt from the RE to SS verification.

The   SS   contains   more information than the RE, particularly   in   the   area   of   data   formats.   Thus   the verification is concerned with showing that the SS is a plausible expansion of the RE, rather than showing that the SS is "correct" with respect to the RE.

In   the   excerpt   names   from the RE have "{RE}" appended   to   make   their   origin clear, and similarly names from the SS have "{SS}" appended to them.

6.1.2   RE to SS Transformation

We   wish   to   show the equivalence between the function   Initiate_Subscriber   {SS}   and   the   action Accept Initial   Schedule   {RE} described earlier in this annex. We start by considering the relevant data items.

Data Item Equivalence

/Init_Sched_Details/   {SS}   corresponds   to Subscribers Initial Schedule {RE}. The format of /Init_Sched _Details/ {SS} is adequate to represent the opening hours so that /Init_Sched_Details/ {SS} is a plausible expansion of Subscribers Initial Schedule {RE}.

//Curr_Sched//   {SS}   corresponds   to   Current Stored   Schedule   {RE}   which   can take the value of Initial Stored   Schedule   {RE}. The format requirements are the same as   for   /Init_Sched_Details/ {SS}. //Curr_Sched// {SS} and /Init_Sched_Details/   {SS}   have   the same format so //Curr_ Sched//   {SS}   is   a   plausible   expansion of Current Stored Schedule {RE}.

///Subs_Active/// {SS} has no counterpart in the RE. We   will   consider   the   use   of this data item when we discuss functional equivalence below.

Function Equivalence

Initiate Subscriber {SS} corresponds to Accept Initial Schedule {RE}. The inputs and outputs correspond as described above except that ///Subs_Active/// {SS} has no counterpart in the RE. Accept Initial Schedule {RE} is defined as a demand action, initiated on input of Subscribers Initial Schedule {RE}. Initiate Subscriber {SS} is also defined as a demand function, triggered by it's input. Thus, from the point of initiation, the action and function are equivalent.

If ///Subs_Active///(/Subs_Id/) {SS} is FALSE when Initiate Subscriber {SS} is initiated, and the input schedule is valid, then ///Subs_Active///(/Subs_Id/) is set TRUE by this function. In this case Initiate Subscriber {SS} also assigns the subscriber identifier and list of opening hours from /Init_Sched_Details/ {SS} to //Curr_Sched// {SS} together with the date and time at which the input was received. The (implicit) transfer function for Accept Initial Schedule {RE} is that:

    Current Stored Schedule {RE}
    := Initial Stored Schedule {RE}
    := Subscribers Initial Schedule {RE}

Thus the transfer functions are equivalent when there is valid input for a genuinely new subscriber.

The transfer function for Initiate Subscriber {SS} shows that if ///Subs_Active///(/Subs_Id/) {SS} is TRUE, or if the input schedule is invalid, then the input is rejected. This is consistent with Subscribers Initial Schedule {RE} being shown as a critical data flow, but Initial Stored Schedule {RE} being shown as non-critical.

Thus we can conclude that Initiate Subscriber {SS} is a plausible expansion of Accept Initial Schedule {RE}.

6.1.3 Commentary

The excerpt above shows the style of the verification process. The later validation steps were slightly more formal and most of them had the form of the "proof outlines" which one might get if producing an informal description of a formal verification process.

In general it was found to be quite difficult to perform some of the verification steps. The step from the SS to the AFS was found to be most difficult due to the change in the structure of the representation. Tool support to the verification process would be very valuable.

Finally it should be noted that our verification merely serves to show that the representations we have produced are satisfactory - it doesn't show that they are in some sense good designs. In the long run it would be desirable to develop criteria for judging the quality of designs, and tools for testing the representations against these criteria, or to help the designer to produce good designs.

6.2 Change Processing Experiment

The change processing experiment is briefly described in section 3.3. The inclusion of an excerpt from [Systems Designers Limited (1982h)] would add little to the understanding of the methods, so we make no further comment on this experiment here.

Annex 2

A general data model for software development and maintenance

1 INTRODUCTION

The following is a first attempt to define a general data model for software development and maintenance. The model is general in the sense that it is independent of specific methods or tools except for the method of configuration control. In this area, the model is influenced by the main ideas of a model implemented in the system SGDL developed by CIT-ALCATEL with the assistance of TECSI-SOFTWARE (Maisonneuve et al. (1981), Maisonneuve (1981), Caillet et al. (1982)) who now market an enhanced product version under the name SDL 2020.

Nevertheless, the model reflects the specific view of development and maintenance elaborated in the technical report of the study. It does certainly not cover all aspects but it tries to give the flavour and provides a basis for discussion. The model contains also some ideas from the Pilot Software Development System (SDS), developed by RSRE-Malvern (SDS (undated)).

1.1 The nature of the description

The description of the model is situated on a level being close to a requirements expression and a specification. It uses a semi-formal graphic notation for an entity-relationship model being derived from the notations developed by the RSRE for the SDS system. The description of the model in this notation is then interpreted in prose to provide the semantics not captured with the notation. The graphic notation has been chosen because it allows to express the necessary details without expressing too much or giving the impression of being formal and because it permits obtaining an overview of the model quite rapidly.

1.2 Notation

The notation is based on a notation developed by the RSRE for the SDS system. It is explained informally with a simple example.

DATA BASE SECTION S1

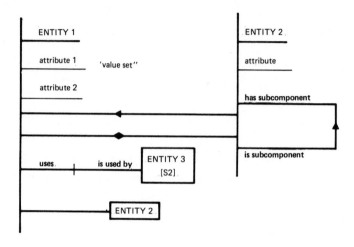

DATA BASE SECTION S2

As the notation is a graphic one it is convenient to structure the whole description into data base sections. This may remain a technical matter. Entities of entity sets have attributes and relationships indicated by horizontal lines emanating from the vertical line underneath an entity set name.

Attributes have names (e.g. attribute 1), and their value sets may or may not be mentioned explicitly.

Relationships between entities are of three kinds : one-to-one (+),
one-to-many (◄─), and many-to-many (◄►─). Computable relationships are
indicated by dotted lines.

A relationship is readable from both sides (e.g. "ENTITY 1 **uses**
ENTITY2" and "ENTITY2 is **used by** ENTITY1"). If it is not possible or inconvenient
to draw a relation line between two vertical entity set lines then an entity set name
is repeated in a rectangle (e.g. | ENTITY2 |). If such an entity set belongs to a
different data base section it is repeated together with the name of its data base
section (e.g. | ENTITY3 |).
| [S2] |

Generally, if details are irrelevant or will not be used later on or are
rather obvious (e.g. complementary names for relationships, value sets) they are
omitted.

In comments on the data model the following notational conventions
will be applied : entity set names are written with capital letters, relationship
names   are   in   bold-face,   attributes   are   enclosed   between   brackets
(e.g. ⟨ management informations⟩), and values of attributes are enclosed between
double quotes.

When   specific   entities   are   used   in   examples   the   values   of
characteristic attributes are given but other attribute values, of no interest in the
example, are omitted. The specific entities are also called by their entity set name.

At the end of section 2.2.1 another notational convention with be
explained which is already used in 2.1 but in a way transparent to the reader.

It   has   been   tried   to   keep   the   text   readable   while   indicating
nevertheless applied occurrences of entity set names, attribute names etc. by
applying the notational conventions.

2 DESCRIPTION

2.1 The Entity / Relationship Model Representation

In this description of the general data model, logical or abstract data items are represented by data base entities or groups of entities with their relationships. The model covers the life cycle activities as it has a uniform view of all the logical data produced and controlled during the life cycle. These logical data are contained in "products". Products are, for instance, the documents of requirements expression, system specification etc. but also the source code and the object code of a module, the executable system, test data etc. In short, the result of any activity producing data is called a product. Sometimes the term "document" is used to refer to the same concept.

The model reflects a specific method of controlling the evolution and configuration of products. As a consequence, a product is represented by a group of entities with their relationships, forming a tree structure, of which the root entity is called a PRODUCT ENTITY.

The reader has to keep in mind these distinctions of logical data item, data base entity, product (as the unit of configuration control), and PRODUCT ENTITY.

The entities of the data model are grouped into four database sections according to the following broad characterization.

Section M deals with the data describing the management of the products produced on a project, i.e. their organization in LIBRARIES and PRODUCT BASES, associated access rights and product visibility.

Section P deals with the data which are the "contents" of a product and those which describe the evolution of a product.

Section G shows the data which characterize the type of a product, the way of producing it and the way of recording its history.

Section O finally deals with the data describing the planning, organization, and status of a project.

These data base sections are shown on the following four pages.

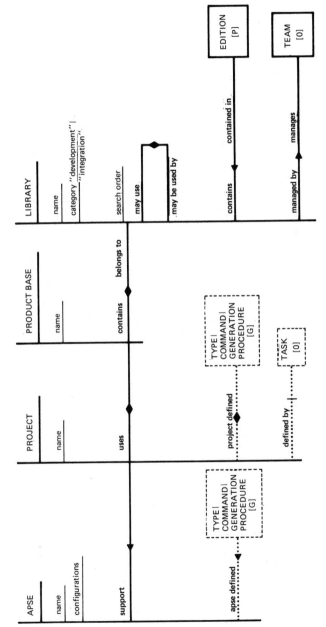

DATA BASE SECTION M (Management)

DATA BASE SECTION P (Product Evolution)

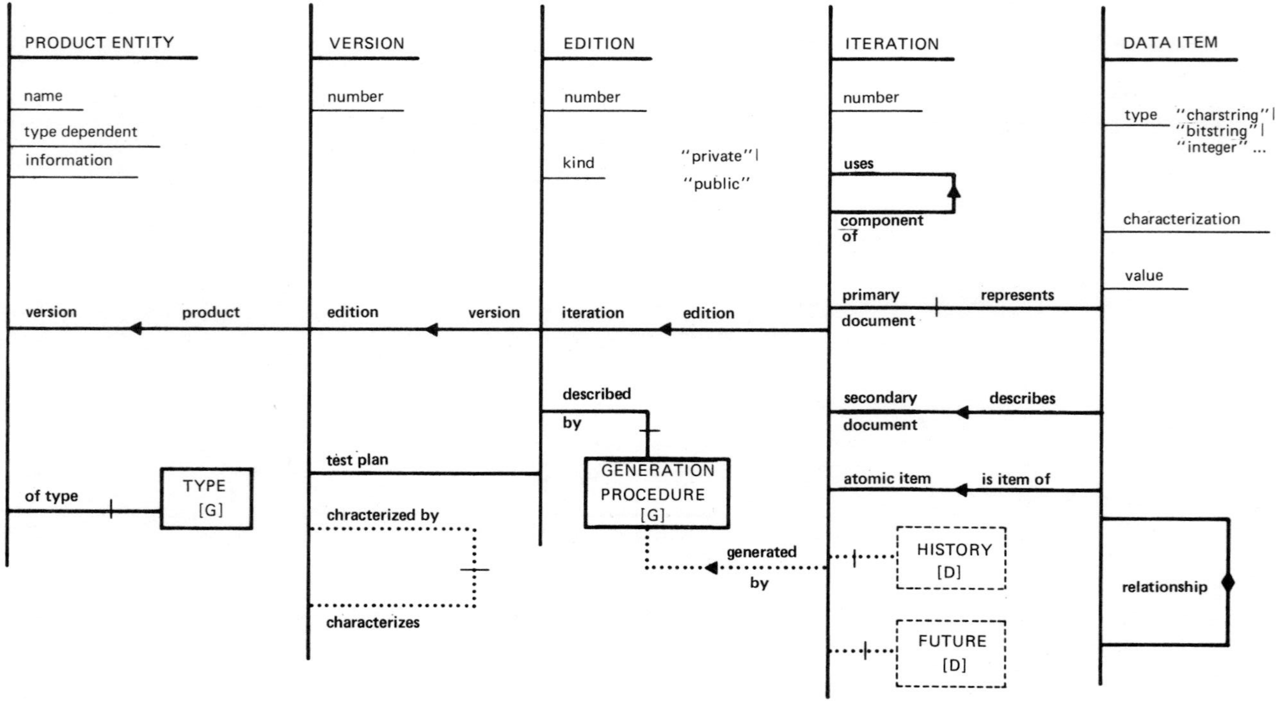

DATA BASE SECTION G (Generation Procedure)

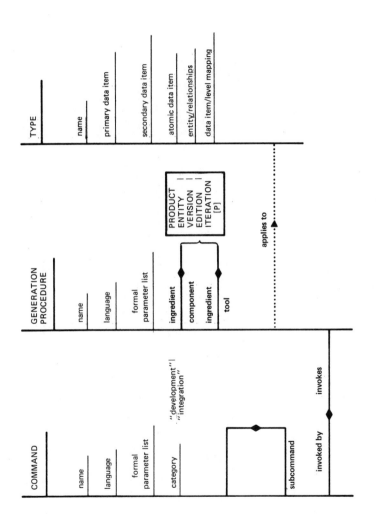

DATA BASE SECTION O (Organisation)

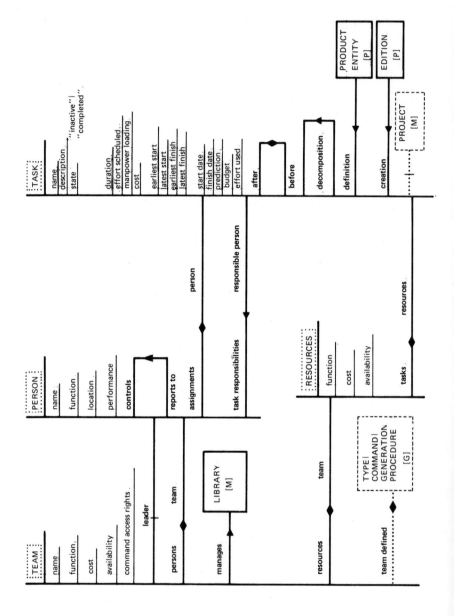

2.2 The interpretation

Every data item produced by a project has to be kept track of (the environment should never "forget"). The configuration control mechanism is in charge of this keeping track, i.e. of identifying the data items and of relating them together according to "their configuration". Hence this mechanism plays a fundamental pervasive role in a support environment.

The method of configuration control considered here is based on the principle that all main data items are considered "products" the evolutionary stages of which are uniquely identified and recorded in a data base of products, called a PRODUCT BASE. Because of the important role of this idea in the data model the following section explains this idea before the whole model is interpreted in detail.

2.2.1 Configuration control records the evolution of a product in its structure. In order to ease the task of interpreting the model, the fundamental product concept is first explained with the help of a simplified view of the data base section P :

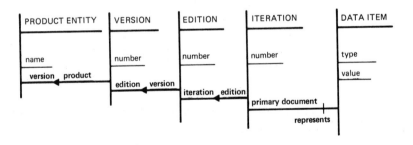

Consider the example of an Ada package A which imports another package B. After compilation, the object code of A is considered a product of type "object". Let its <name> be "A.OBJ". Similary "B.OBJ" may be the product "object code of B". The first important observation is that the DATA ITEM which is the object code is distinguished from the PRODUCT ENTITY which it represents. Yet, there are even three intermediate entities. The second important observation is that a product has the structure of a tree considering only the above relationships.

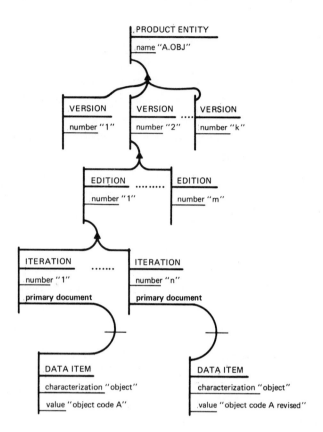

The DATA ITEMS (characterization "object") are **primary documents representing** each a uniquely identified "incarnation" of the product, i.e. a certain **iteration** of an **edition** of a **version** of the PRODUCT ENTITY.

The unique numbering is the task of the configuration control system which records the evolution of products. The intermediate levels reflect the reasons for which there may be different "incarnations" of a product.

The VERSION level reflects functional changes in the product. Such a functional change would occur, for instance when the package A changes its specification slightly by offering another operation.

The EDITION level reflects changes in the composition of a **version** of the PRODUCT ENTITY. An example of such a change is that package A imports a new **version** of B.

The ITERATION level finally reflects simple revisions of the object code of A, e.g., editorial changes which do not change the functionality nor the composition.

Hence, what is traditionally called a "product", e.g. the object code of package A, is, seen through the lenses of a general and powerful configuration control model, the DATA ITEM **representing** an **iteration** of an **edition** of a **version** of a PRODUCT ENTITY.

However, in many cases, it is desirable to make an abstraction from a specific incarnation of a product, i.e. not to talk about just one path in the above product tree from the PRODUCT ENTITY to a DATA ITEM **representing** the specific incarnation.

By identifying a product only up to a certain level in its product tree one can express an invariance against the product evolution on the levels non-specified. An appropriate default rule may complete such an "incomplete" reference where a complete reference is required.

This abstraction mechanism is essential to the configuration control method and heavily exploited. In fact, most relationships between products will generally exist on a higher level than the ITERATION level.

By making the level of references subject to definition it is possible to define the level on which a change in a certain product affects another product with which it has a relationship.

Wherever a complete reference to a product is required it will be indicated explicitly.

More notational conventions related to the product concept : where the "product structure" is not focussed upon it will be made transparent in various ways. For instance, the chain of relationships will be omitted, and the DATA ITEM **representing** an **iteration** of an **edition** of a **version** of a PRODUCT ENTITY **of type** "object" with < name> "A.OBJ" is called either way

-        the **primary document** of an **iteration** of PRODUCT ENTITY...
-        the **primary document** of an ITERATION of...
-        the **primary document** of product "A.OBJ"
-        the product "A.OBJ"

of course only where no ambiguity arises.

Furthermore, a DATA ITEM with   name   "A" and < characterization> "object" will also be referred to as the OBJECT with <name> "A". Similary, a product with a PRODUCT ENTITY **of type** TYPE where TYPE has the name "object" is referred to as an OBJECT.

This shorthand has already been used in data base section O. The entity set names in boxes drawn with dotted lines are products. Therefore,

is a shorthand for :

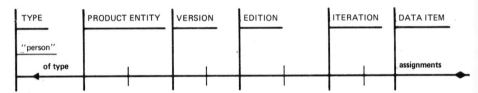

TYPE	PRODUCT ENTITY	VERSION	EDITION	ITERATION	DATA ITEM
"person"					assignments

2.2.1   <u>Management of products (section M)</u>. PROJECTS are **supported by** the APSE which offers a basic set of **APSE-defined** COMMANDS, **APSE-defined** TYPES describing standard products, and **APSE-defined** GENERATION PROCEDURES for generating these standard products.

The APSE has furthermore a < name> and its < configuration> is described.

A PROJECT has the TASK to develop and/or maintain a software system consisting of many components of different "nature", "status" and "history" which are all considered products regardless of their complexity.

This TASK is therefore a complex one which will generally be recursively decomposed. With each TASK, the corresponding products are associated. TASKS are assigned to PERSONS who belong to a TEAM.

Products play a central role in the project; they are at the same time essential ingredients as well as results of the work represented by a TASK. On a large project, it has therefore to be stated clearly whose responsibility it is to generate a product and who may make use of it.

The following remarks on the entity sets TEAM, LIBRARY and PRODUCT BASE explain the model as to the access rights to products and the sharing mechanisms. These remarks are crucial for the understanding of the configuration control method. They are non-trivial due to the particular product structure of the model.

It should be clearly defined for each of the products who is responsible for it at a given point in time. In the proposed model, the responsibility for a certain set of products is given to a TEAM in the following way. Each **edition** of a **version** of a PRODUCT ENTITY belongs to exactly one LIBRARY. Each LIBRARY is **managed by** one TEAM. A TEAM is therefore responsible for the products **contained in** the LIBRARIES which are **managed by** the TEAM.

As a consequence, no two TEAMS are responsible for the same unique ITERATION or EDITION of a product. Since (as will be discussed below) a GENERATION PROCEDURE is linked to an EDITION of a PRODUCT ENTITY this means that a specific "generation right" belongs to exactly one TEAM. It has the right to modify the GENERATION PROCEDURE.

On the other hand, a PRODUCT ENTITY and its **versions** can be shared by different TEAMS if the former are **contained in** different LIBRARIES **managed by** the latter.

TEAMS generally have specific < functions>: program development, integration, testing, administration etc. functions. These functions are reflected in the < category > attribute of the LIBRARIES belonging to the TEAMS. The right of "using" products of other TEAMS is now expressed by the relationships **may use products of** between LIBRARIES.

GENERATION PROCEDURES of a "testing" TEAM may execute or read programs which are products **contained in** a "development" LIBRARY **managed by** a "development" TEAM.

In order to manage the visibility of products in a more flexible way, a < search order> may be specified for a LIBRARY which prescribes the order in which LIBRARIES have to be searched for a product.

Unique identification of products implies the existence of a name space in which this identification takes place.

Since TEAMS and even PROJECTS should be able to share uniquely identified products, this name space must "encompass" the products of several TEAMS, and even PROJECTS, in order to achieve a reasonable configuration control.

Therefore, the model proposes the entity of a PRODUCT BASE to stand for the space of uniquely identified products which are eventually **contained in** all the LIBRARIES which **belong to** a given PRODUCT BASE.

Since the name space is in principle infinite a PRODUCT BASE will never be filled up unless the name space becomes finite by the imposing of limits on the numbering and naming of products and versions etc.

Simplifying, one may say that a PRODUCT BASE is constituted by the products of a set of LIBRARIES. These products can be made available or searched for from all the LIBRARIES **belonging to** the PRODUCT BASE.

Hence, the concept of the PRODUCT BASE allows different projects of development and maintenance to exist independently and simultaneously in the same APSE.

Within a given PROJECT, the use of several PRODUCT BASES allows to coordinate independent developments which may use several common PRODUCTS as illustrated by the following picture.

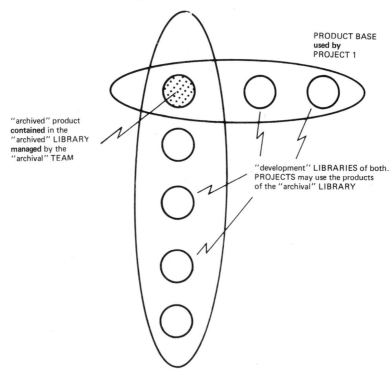

PRODUCT BASE
used by
PROJECT 1

"archived" product
contained in the
"archived" LIBRARY
managed by the
"archival" TEAM

"development" LIBRARIES of both.
PROJECTS may use the products
of the "archival" LIBRARY

PRODUCT BASE **used by** PROJECT 2

On both PROJECTS the unique identification of all products is assured. Hence the names of archived products cannot clash with those of other products.

As well as they may be **APSE-defined,** COMMANDS, TYPES and GENERATION PROCEDURES may also be **project-defined** and **team-defined.** For each TEAM, specific < COMMAND access rights> may be specified.

2.2.3 <u>Data characterising the production (section G)</u>. A GENERATION PROCEDURE defines how the **edition** of a **version** of a PRODUCT ENTITY is generated. A GENERATION PROCEDURE may **invoke** a COMMAND.

The GENERATION PROCEDURE contains references to **ingredient components** and **ingredient tools** which will be used as ingredients in an actual invocation of the GENERATION PROCEDURE.

Such an invocation **generates** an ITERATION of a PRODUCT ENTITY which **is of the type** TYPE to which the GENERATION PROCEDURE applies. It may be (and will normally be) generic in the sense that it is independent of the evolution of the ingredients. It therefore may specify the **ingredient components** and **tools** only down to a certain level in their product tree, i.e. their identification may be incomplete, e.g. only mentioning a PRODUCT ENTITY, a VERSION, or an EDITION.

The GENERATION PROCEDURE is a generic "derivation" in the terminology of the Ada Support System Study (Systems Designers Ltd. et al. (1979)).

Once more, this means that unless one specifies an **ingredient tool** or **component** name completely, a GENERATION PROCEDURE is not changed when the tool or component referenced this way evolves.

The **ingredient tools** and **components** of a specific derivation must, however, be specific ones. The COMMANDS **invoked** by a GENERATION PROCEDURE may therefore use a default mechanism to interpret the "incomplete" identification in order to arrive at a uniquely identified product. A typical default mechanism is to use the last **iteration** of the last **edition** of the last **version** of a PRODUCT ENTITY.

Ingredient tools and **components** may be provided in the < parameter list> of the GENERATION PROCEDURE or as data local to it.

The execution of a GENERATION PROCEDURE **generates** two entities, the HISTORY and the FUTURE of the ITERATION **generated.** The HISTORY will at the end contain the closure of all the specific ingredients in the production. The FUTURE is only set up as the future receptacle for references to unique products for which the ITERATION **generated** will be an **ingredient component.**

The entity-relationships involving the entities HISTORY and FUTURE make the derivation history recording and using more explicit. Where this explicitness is not needed these entity-relationships will simply be replaced by the following :

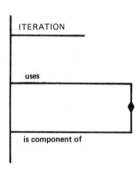

This uses relationship between ITERATIONS underlines once more that specific **ingredient tools** and **components** are completely and uniquely identified.

A COMMAND may be of a specific < category>.

It may also invoke other COMMANDS. As it is the case for the GENERATION PROCEDURE, it may, of course, also have a < parameter list>.

Both, COMMAND and GENERATION-PROCEDURE may be written in a suitable < language>.

Among the **APSE-defined** COMMANDS are at least all those necessary for the administration of PRODUCT BASES and LIBRARIES (e.g. "define product base", "define library", "delete library"), and for the management of products (e.g. for creation, modification - concerning the GENERATION PROCEDURE -, deletion, displaying of **primary documents,** transfer between TEAMS). An important **APSE-defined** COMMAND "verify" checks whether a given product uses the most recent ITERATION of all its **component** products. This COMMAND is used to detect necessary change propagations and will, therefore, be heavily used by management tools.

Each PRODUCT ENTITY   is **of a type** which describes the kind of information which represents the product (cf. next section).

2.2.4 The Product Data (Section P). Many remarks have necessarily already been made about the product data (data base section P) in the previous sections since the product concept is designed to satisfy the needs of configuration control which is a basic underlying activity in an environment.

These remarks, notably of section 2.2.1, are not repeated here but complemented.

A software system is not just a set of products but it has of course a structure which is given by the relationships of its products. The basic relations are the product/**component** product relation and the **use** relation. An ITERATION **uses** other ITERATIONS which are **components** of it. (These latter relationships have been introduced in 2.2.3 as a simplification of the relationships involving the entities HISTORY and FUTURE.)

VERSIONS correspond to functional variants of a product. The variations in functionality have to be documented. For this purpose, a VERSION is **characterized by** a VERSION which may be a document expressing and/or justifying the functional changes.

On the VERSION level, one also has to find the **test plan** which may exist in different EDITIONS according to the **editions** of the VERSION.

It may be useful to distinguish two < kinds > of EDITIONS, "private" ones and "public" ones. Using this attribute as a significant one for identification, allows for an enlargement of the name space and the coexistence of "old" reference PRODUCTS and newly developed ones. The "public" EDITIONS could be in an "archival" PRODUCT BASE overlapping with the one of a current development.

The "contents" of a specific ITERATION of a product consists of one or several DATA ITEMS. Each DATA ITEM has a < type > in the conventional programming language sense and a < value > . It may also have another < characterization   and **relationships** with other DATA ITEMS.

One DATA ITEM is described as the< primary data item> of a TYPE. It corresponds to the **primary document** of an ITERATION. E.g., the **primary document representing** a PRODUCT ENTITY which is **of type** TYPE with < name> "Ada object" is the DATA ITEM with < type> "bit-string" having as its < value > the object code itself.

Other DATA ITEMS may be described as < secondary data items> of a TYPE. They may correspond to the secondary documents of an ITERATION. E.g. **secondary documents** of an "Ada object" may be DATA ITEMS of < type> "bit-string" having as their <value> a symbol table and an intermediate representation, resp., and a DATA ITEM of <type> "document" having as its <value> a human-readable intermediate representation (e.g. in DIANA notation).

Finally, several DATA ITEMS may be described as <atomic data items> of a TYPE together with their <entity relationships>. These DATA ITEMS correspond to the **atomic** items of an ITERATION. They may be the grains detected by a microscopic view of a **primary document** or a **secondary document**. E.g. for an "Ada object" specific symbol table items may be **atomic items** of the ITERATION.

In general, DATA ITEMS may have relationships not only with ITERATIONS but also with EDITIONS, VERSIONS and PRODUCT ENTITIES. These relationships are not shown in the data model in order not to clutter it up. However the attribute <data item/level mapping> of TYPE is shown which defines the association of certain DATA ITEMS with entities on the different levels of the product structure.

To give an example, certain test data may very well reside in a secondary document at the level of a VERSION or an EDITION since this is the logical place of association.

Moreover, there may also be products for which ITERATIONS do not exist as they do not make sense. Such products are in general products which are generated the same way all the time without changing ingredient components and tools. An example is a source text. Even if the editor changes, this does not matter for the text ; therefore the editor need not be mentioned in the GENERATION PROCEDURE (unless, of course, it inserts specific data in the source).

It is the TYPE a PRODUCT ENTITY is of which defines these peculiarities of a certain product.

2.2.5 The Project Data (Section 0). A project **is defined by** a TASK. Since a TASK may again be **decomposed** into TASKS the TASK **defining** the PROJECT may be the root of a TASK hierarchy. Each TASK of this hierarchy demands the production of one or more products. Each TASK is assigned to one or more PERSONS. If it is assigned to several PERSONS one of them has the **responsibility** for the TASK. The PERSONS working on the TASK of a PROJECT belong each to a TEAM. One of the persons of a TEAM is its **leader.** There are PERSONS **controlling** other PERSONS, and PERSONS **reporting to** other PERSONS. Finally there are RESOURCES which are allocated to TASKS and hence to TEAMS.

The entities TEAM, PERSON, TASK and RESOURCE all have the product structure so that their evolution in time can be recorded and controlled in the same way as that of the software products under development.

A TEAM has a < name> , a < function> (with possible values "development", "integration", "test", etc.), a < cost> of operation, and an < availability> . It **manages** one or more LIBRARIES, and has specific < command access rights> .

A PERSON has a < name> and a < function> . He works at a < location> , and his < performance> may be recorded.

With a RESOURCE, the attributes < name> ,< function> ,< cost> of using it, and < availability> are associated.

The most elaborate entity is the TASK which has a large number of attributes describing its planning and its status.   < name>, < description> , **definition** and **creation** of products, and **decomposition** characterize the objectives of a TASK. Its **after** and **before** relationships with other TASKS show its logical dependencies. < duration> , < effort scheduled> , < man-power> loading and < cost > are the (redundant) parameters for the planning. The planning is reflected by the < earliest start> , < latest start> , and < earliest finish> , < latest finish > attributes.

The progress on a TASK is monitored with the help of the attributes < start-date> , < finish date> , < fixed-finish> , < predictions> , < budget > , and < effort used> . A task is in an "inactive" state when no effort is devoted to it.

3 MAIN OPERATIONS OF CONFIGURATION CONTROL

Chapter 2 has only occasionally hinted at the operations on the data described by the data model.

The development operations on the data consist mainly in the generation of products and the analysis of their data.

Examples of the entity/relationships representing the contents of various products are given in Annex 3.

The operations of project management on the data describing the planning, organization and status of a project have been described above in the main body of this book (cf.3.1.8).

In this section, the main operations of configuration control and integration management are shortly presented since they have motivated most aspects of the data model.

3.1 Setting up of a project

Initialization of a project for configuration control and integration means establishing LIBRARIES and PRODUCT BASES, setting up **project-defined** and **team-defined** COMMANDS, TYPES and GENERATION PROCEDURES, and assigning the < Command access   rights > to the TEAMS according to their < function>.

Imagine the example of a PROJECT which is to develop a new version of a system already delivered and archived. The development TEAMS should be able to access the archived version until the products of the new version emerge and have to be integrated progressively.

PRODUCT BASES and LIBRARIES could be defined as follows :

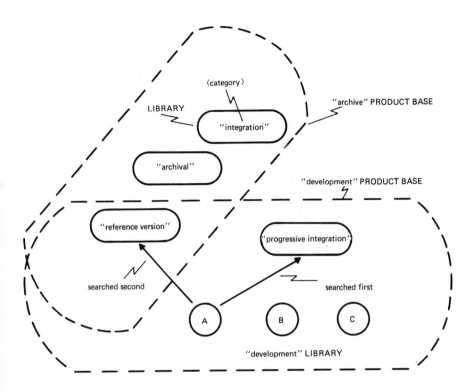

Each of the "development" LIBRARIES may **use products of** the "reference version" LIBRARY and the "progressive integration" LIBRARY but the products of the latter LIBRARY should be preferred. This is to be expressed appropriately by the < search order> of the "development" LIBRARY.

3.2 Definition and creation of products

Definition and creation of a product have to be distinguished. The definition creates the entities PRODUCT, VERSION and EDITION, evaluates these attributes and establishes the relationships concerning the product structure and the TYPE. The creation invokes the GENERATION PROCEDURE, generates the DATA ITEMS of an ITERATION and evaluates the corresponding attributes and relationships. Hence, the definition is a kind of stub definition, the creation replaces the stub by an incarnation.

PRODUCT ENTITY   name   and VERSION   number   are explicitly defined by the TEAMS according to the PROJECT conventions. EDITION < number> and ITERATION < number > are controlled by the configuration control system. They are incremented whenever a new GENERATION PROCEDURE is defined and a new ITERATION is generated, respectively.

"Definition" and "creation" could be explicit **APSE-defined** COMMANDS, they could as well be **subcommands** of other COMMANDS which represent a less abstract interface to the APSE-User.

3.3 Exchanging products

There should be at least four different mechanisms for exchanging products.

- "copy definition":

The PRODUCT ENTITY and VERSION level (and possibly the EDITION level in case of a "public" EDITION kind are copied to another LIBRARY or PRODUCT BASE, i.e. the stub definition is created which is necessary for subsequent creation of a product. In this case the EDITION < number> is incremented.

-"transfer":

The responsibility for a given product is "transferred" from one LIBRARY to another within a PRODUCT BASE, i.e. the relationships **is managed by** and **manages** change. (No duplication of the product tree or of DATA ITEMS need happen.) The transfer should be done by a TEAM which has the < function> "integration" or "progressive integration" and generally not by the "development" TEAM having managed the product to be transferred.

- "save":

A product together with all its related entities and all its component products (recursively) is completely copied without a change of identification of any product involved, into a different PRODUCT BASE.

- "regenerate":

A product (which may be a total system) is completely regenerated, generally under the responsibility of an "archival" TEAM and with resulting EDITIONS of < kind > "public".

Saving and regeneration should be two-step processes with a validation step checking for most-recentness and completeness before the actual saving or regeneration step. If a product to be regenerated contains "public" EDITIONS regeneration of these EDITIONS may not be necessary if they exist already in the "archive" PRODUCT BASE.

The rationale for these four exchange mechanisms is given in the next section where the working mechanism of a PROJECT is considered.

3.4 The working of a project

Consider the example of a PROJECT mentioned in 3.1 and illustrated on the next page. The "archival" LIBRARY **contains** the VERSION < number> "2" of a product **of type** "system". "Development TEAMS" **managing** LIBRARIES A, B, C, are assigned the tasks of designing and coding a new VERSION "3" of the given system according to existing specifications. The archived version has EDITIONS of kind "public" indicating an official version. After the PROJECT has been set up, the "reference version"< number > "2" has to be made visible for the "development" LIBRARIES. It is therefore transferred. (Step 1 on the next page).

The TEAMS **managing** LIBRARIES A, B, C may now copy the definitions of products they have to modify, and then work on the creation of the new VERSION "3" for these products (2). The new VERSION of a product may progressively be integrated after a transfer to the "progressive integration" LIBRARY (3). The progressive integration makes the new reference products more and more visible. They replace the old reference products due to the < search order > of the "development" LIBRARIES (cf.3.1).

At the end of integration tests, the new system version is saved, i.e. completely copied to the "integration" LIBRARY in the "archive" PRODUCT BASE (4). Thus having all the necessary ingredients with their unique identification as well as all the GENERATION PROCEDURES, the "archival" TEAM **managing** the "archival" LIBRARY regenerates the complete system with "public" EDITIONS. Validation tests follow the successful system regeneration. In the validation part of step (4) of "saving" the new system version it is checked that the new version is built using the most recently developed ITERATIONS. The data necessary for such a check by the **APSE-defined** COMMAND "verify" have obviously been recorded in the product data.

The advantage of distinguishing "private" and "public" EDITIONS is two-fold. It is easily recognizable which products archived have been used in a new development without any changes, and redelivering or regenerating archived products can be avoided.

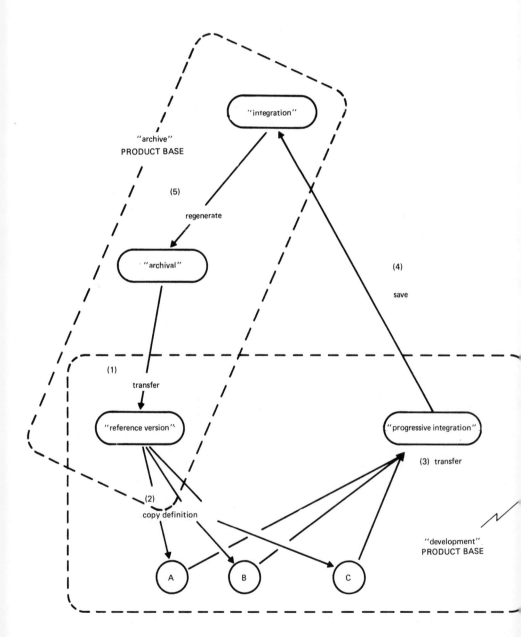

Annex 3

Microscopic views of life cycle
documents and configuration control

1 INTRODUCTION

In chapter 2.2.3 of the main body of the book on the overall requirements for a coherent APSE, the distinction between a macroscopic and a microscopic view of documents has been introduced. The macroscopic view is simply understood as looking at a document as a whole, the microscopic view is looking into a document and discovering internal structure. The grain size of the elements of the internal structure may, of course, vary to a large degree. There could be various levels of structure. The general data model presented in Annex 2 allows for both views to be taken in parallel. It provides for DATA ITEMS which are **primary documents** and **secondary documents** of an ITERATION (macroscopic view) and for DATA ITEMS, which are **atomic items** of an ITERATION (microscopic view). These atomic DATA ITEMS may have relationships between them as defined by the < atomic data items> and < entity relationships> of the TYPE of the corresponding products.

In this annex, possible microscopic views of four **primary documents** of major life cycle products are given.

These documents are the Requirements Expression (RE), System Specification (SS), Abstract Functional Specification (AFS) and Module Decomposition (MD) documents corresponding to the development methods investigated in this book.

It is then briefly discussed how the relationships of atomic DATA ITEMS may be controlled accross product boundaries.

2 EXAMPLES OF MICROSCOPIC VIEWS

2.1 The representation of atomic data items

It is recalled how the general data model introduced **atomic items** of ITERATIONS:

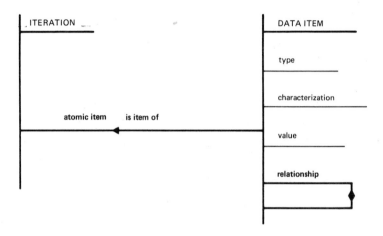

For a PRODUCT ENTITY **of type** TYPE the latter describes the attributes of the specific atomic data items and their **relationships :**

```
TYPE

  atomic data item

  entity relationships
```

(These attributes of TYPE may only be known to an analysis tool which produces the microscopic view from a **primary document** or **secondary document** of the PRODUCT.)

The entity/relationship models in the following sections correspond to the values of the above attributes of the TYPES "RE", "SS", "AFS" and "MD", respectively.

Each of the entities is an interpretation of a DATA ITEM in the general model and hence an **item of** an ITERATION.

The attribute < name>, usually present, has been omitted from the pictures.

2.2 Requirements Expression

The entity/relationship model is quite simple and should be self explanatory. Interesting are the "forward relationships" to the atomic DATA ITEMS of the System Specification (SS). (These may not apply in the case of DATA, ACTIONS and VIEWPOINTS of the OPERATIONAL REQUIREMENTS.)

DATA BASE SECTION RE (Requirements Expression)

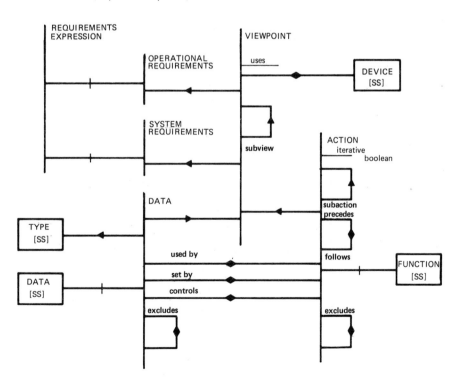

2.3 System Specification

The System Specification mainly deals with FUNCTIONS, DATA, TYPES and DEVICES. It should also document decisions (DESCRIPTION/JUSTIFICATIONS) and note EXPECTED CHANGES. TYPES and DATA may reference DATA of the Requirements Expression. FUNCTIONS have their origin in ACTIONS of the Requirements Expression and may give rise to FUNCTIONS of the Abstract Functional Specification. A DEVICE may backreference a VIEW POINT.

DATA BASE SECTION SS (System Specification)

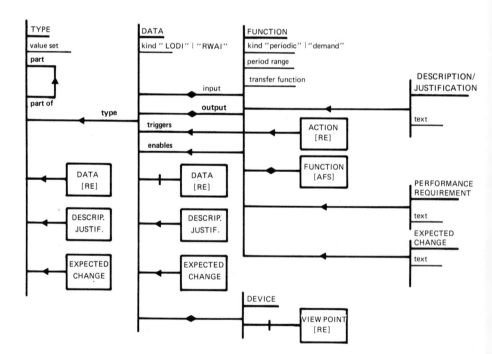

2.4 Abstract Functional Specification

The Abstract Functional Specification (AFS) expresses a language independent system design. It specifies the internal working of system functions, and the data flows within the system.

FUNCTIONS with FORMAL PARAMETERS have **usages** as FUNCTION INSTANCES. DATA ITEMS of the kinds LODI (Logical Data Item), RWAI (Real World Available Item), and global and local IDI (Internal Data Item) are **actual parameters.**

The attributes of the DATA ITEMS and the FORMAL PARAMETERS are the same as in the System Specification and therefore not repeated in the following picture.

Backward references may for instance be made to FUNCTIONS of the System Specifications and forward references to MODULES and FUNCTIONS of the Module Decomposition (MD) and the Module Specification (MS).

DATA BASE SECTION AFS (Abstract Functional Specification)

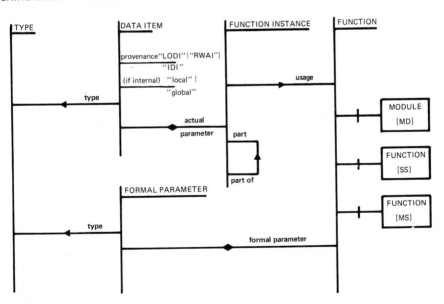

2.5 Module Decomposition

The Module Decomposition document is part of the Module Specification document.

It is an example where the "microscopic" grains are quite large. MODULES and SECRETS could very well be described in more details. There are forward references to DATA and PROGRAM UNITS of Module Specifications (MS).

As a MODULE may be in a relationship with FUNCTIONS on the Abstract Functional Specification level and these again with FUNCTIONS and ACTIONS of the System Specification and Requirements Expression resp., the views given here illustrate well the life cycle model with its lines connecting representations of different levels. Such relationship chains may be exploited by various analysis tools.

DATA BASE SECTION MD (Module Decomposition)

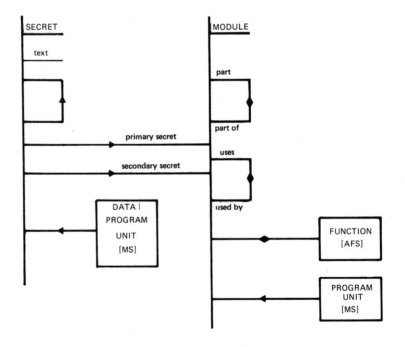

3 EVOLUTION OF ATOMIC DATA ITEM RELATIONSHIPS

In the main body of the book (cf.3.2.1.2), it has been indicated that we do not know a satisfactory solution to the problem of complete configuration control of atomic data items. By "complete control" we mean a control which does not merely rely on the evolution of enclosing documents of large grain size.

Here we are going to demonstrate briefly how the evolution of atomic data items can be controlled with respect to the enclosing product, i.e. by considering the enclosing product as being modified whenever one of its microscopic data items is being changed.

The interesting chain of inter-document relationships between the atomic data items ACTIONS, FUNCTIONS, and even PROGRAM UNITS of the products RE, SS, AFS, MD and MS provide a good example for the discussion.

Imagine the probably most frequent case of a change which has to be propagated "top-down", i.e. from left to right in our life cycle model. (The argumentation is analogous in the bottom-up case.) The products RE, SS and AFS may exist in specific ITERATIONS, as shown by the picture, and analysis tools may have established the relationships between the atomic data items A, F and G.

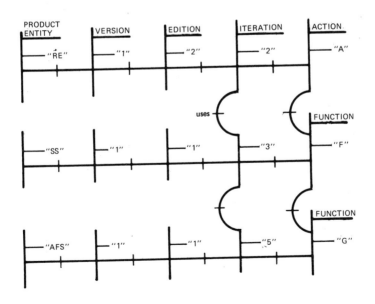

We have to consider the triggering of a change propagation, the nature of the changes, and the halt of the propagation.

A change propagation is triggered when the **uses** relationship of a product's ITERATION does no more reference the latest ITERATION of a used product.

Imagine that the RE of our example is revised to give the third ITERATION. This ITERATION is not **used by** the ITERATION 3 of SS. Therefore, the change in RE has to be propagated to SS.

One way to update SS could now be the complete (macroscopic) refabrication of SS using the latest ITERATION of RE. But this would mean not exploiting the microscopic information at all.

Due to this detailed information, the effect of the RE-change on SS may be analyzed and localized. Assume, the change of RE has only changed the action A and that only the function F of SS can be affected by this change.

If F has to be changed then this leads to a new ITERATION of SS, either by complete refabrication or partial refabrication and copying. If F need not be changed then no new ITERATION of SS is generated. In either case, however, something has to be done about the relationship between A and F, depending on its implementation. If it is implemented by direct pointers then pointers have to be copied even if SS is not to be revised.

A better implementation may be one which considers a reference to an atomic data item as a pair (name of item, product reference specified up to its EDITION). Then, before the revision of RE, F would reference ("A", RE/**version** 1/**edition** 2). This reference would still be valid after the propagation of the change to SS.

Finally, the change propagation comes to a halt when no new ITERATION is generated. For example, when SS is not revised a change propagation to AFS is not triggered. The following picture summarizes the discussion schematically.

RE/version 1/edition 2/iteration 2   RE/1/2/3

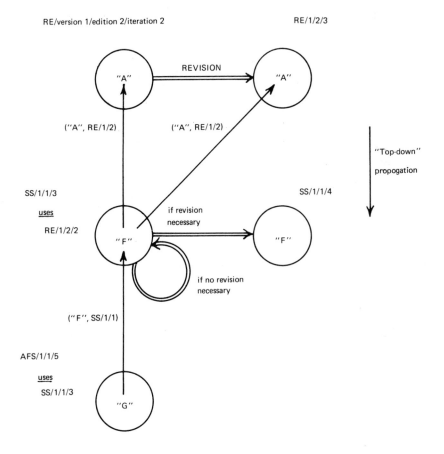

4 CONCLUSION

The microscopic view of documents together with relationships across life cycle levels opens up interesting possibilities for analysis, change impact assessment, estimation techniques, automatic generation, information retrieval, etc.

It increases the coherence between methods and tools and is the true sign of an integrated environment.

This approach poses, however, a couple of problems.

The number of relationships probably grows exponentially with decreasing "grain" size so that an acceptable grain size has to be found.

New database mechanisms may have to be developed in order to manage the software system database with a reasonable performance.

Since the life cycle activities demand human ingenuity at each level, references across levels can, in general, not be inferred automatically. The effectiveness of a true integration in the above sense will therefore always depend on the discipline of the human involved who has to provide explicit cross-references.

He will provide these more readily if the "grains" are large. He could, of course, always be assisted in his effort by a suitable prompting mechanism built into the generation tools he is using.

Annex 4

Examples of current practice

1 INTRODUCTION

In this annex five examples of current practice are illustrated. The intention is solely to give a general indication of the main features of each method. The presentations for three of the methods are based on a fairly brief study of the methods, or on informal discussions with the originators. The originators of these methods have not had the opportunity to check and correct our presentations, so the presentations must be regarded as illustrating our understanding of the methods, rather than being definitive descriptions of the methods. In any event many of the methods are still evolving so our presentations may, by now, be out of date.

Despite these caveats we believe that this annex is interesting and useful as it attempts to describe the methods within a common framework, and this helps in understanding the methods, at a gross level, and with comparing the methods at this level.

232

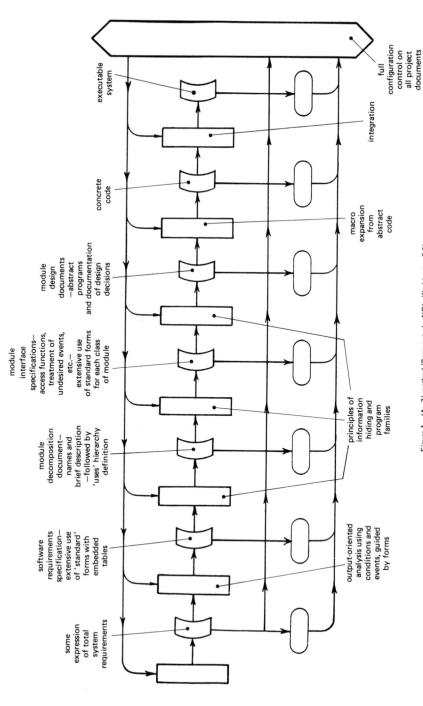

Figure 1 'A—7' method (Parnas et al., NRL, Washington DC)

2   A-7 METHOD

The "A-7 method" was developed by Parnas and his colleagues at the Naval Research Laboratory, Washington, D.C., for the redesign of the software for the A-7 aircraft [Heninger et al (1978)]. This method is illustrated in Figure 1. Key aspects of the methods are an emphasis on rigorous documents, the central role played by the "Software Requirements Specification" (upon which all subsequent development is based), and the use of rigorous module interface specifications. The major principles employed include information hiding [Parnas (1972)], program families [Parnas (1976)], disciplined programming [Dijkstra (1976)], and a general emphasis on "pragmatic formality". These various principles provide constructive guidance during program development.

Some form of verification at every stage is an integral part of the overall method. With a series of rigorous documents and extensive use of "standard" forms and tables there is a basis for completeness and consistency checking within documents, and consistency checking between documents. Similarly the rigorous module specifications provide a basis for module testing using conventional techniques, and could if desired be employed for formal verification.

It should be noted that the Naval Research Laboratory project is concerned with the redesign of existing software, and therefore the overall expression of system requirements is given by existing documents, to some extent. However it would seem that for completely new developments some means of capturing requirements in a form that is compatible with the methods currently in use would be both possible and desirable.

234

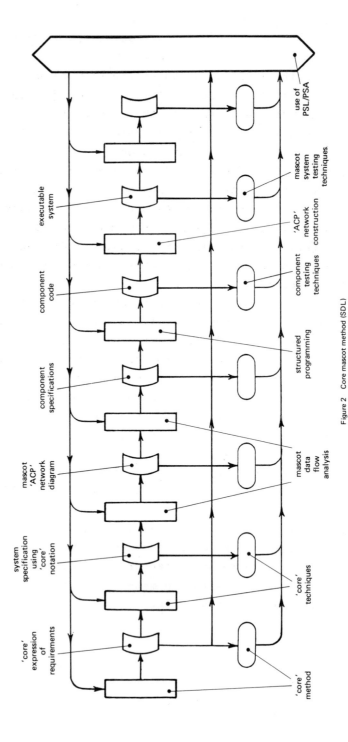

Figure 2   Core mascot method (SDL)

3   CORE/MASCOT

The   CORE/MASCOT method is illustrated in Figure
2. CORE [Systems Designers Limited (1978)] was developed
within Systems Designers Limited. MASCOT was developed at
the Royal Signals and Radar Establishment, Malvern, England
and is now a standard method of the U.K. Ministry of
Defence. Simple development environments supporting the
MASCOT method of software development have been developed by
a number of firms, and are now commercially available. The
CORE/MASCOT combination [Augusta (1981)] was established in
collaborative work by Systems Designers Limited and British
Aerospace.

CORE is primarily aimed at requirements
expression, although it is possible to use the CORE
techniques and notation for system specification, and this
approach is reflected in Figure 2. CORE is described in much
more detail in Chapter 3 and Annex 1 in it's requirements
analysis role.

MASCOT addresses the development of systems
which display a disciplined approach to concurrency and a
useful degree of modularity. The components of a MASCOT
system are identified by a process of data flow analysis and
by applying general principles of encapsulation. MASCOT
components and systems are normally verified by use of
conventional testing techniques, with certain MASCOT-
specific techniques being employed for system integration.

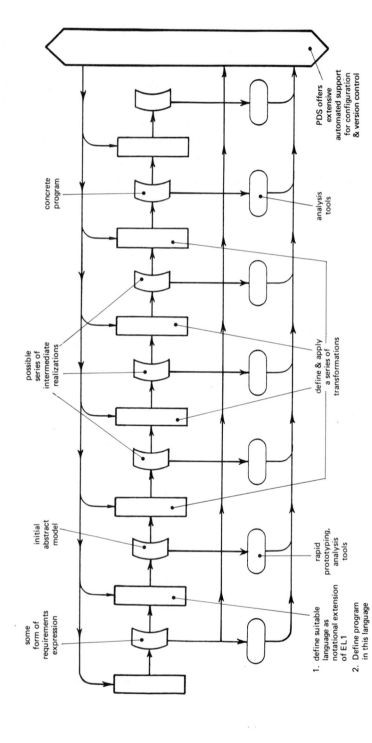

some form of requirements expression

initial abstract model

possible series of intermediate realizations

concrete program

1. define suitable language as notational extension of EL1
2. Define program in this language

rapid prototyping, analysis tools

define & apply a series of transformations

analysis tools

PDS offers extensive automated support for configuration & version control

Figure 3   PDS method (Cheatham et al., Harvard)

4   PDS METHOD

Figure 3 illustrates the PDS developed by Cheatham and his colleagues at Harvard University.

The PDS is based upon an approach called Transformational Refinement [Cheatham et al (1981)]. In order to produce a program one first envisages an "ideal" language in which to express the program. This language is used to produce an abstract model of the desired program, which is then refined by a series of transformations until a concrete (executable) program is produced.

In PDS, the "ideal" language for the given problem is actually defined by notational extension of the ELl programming language. A separate formal language is used to define the transformations to be applied at each stage. The transformations are actually applied by the PDS tools, with automated version and configuration control to retain consistency in the event of subsequent change to either the abstract program or the tranformation definitions.

Two of the key features of PDS are the use of rapid prototyping and the extensive use of analysis tools. A rapid prototype can be produced from the initial abstract model by using "naive" transformations which would not be suitable for production use, but which are suitable for purposes of investigation. Experience gained from the rapid prototype might suggest modifications to the abstract model and will guide the definition of the transformations. Available analysis tools include tracing, performance monitoring, and a generalised data flow analyser. A prototype symbolic evaluation tool has been implemented, and a production version is under construction. All of the PDS tools are cosely integrated into the overall PDS environment.

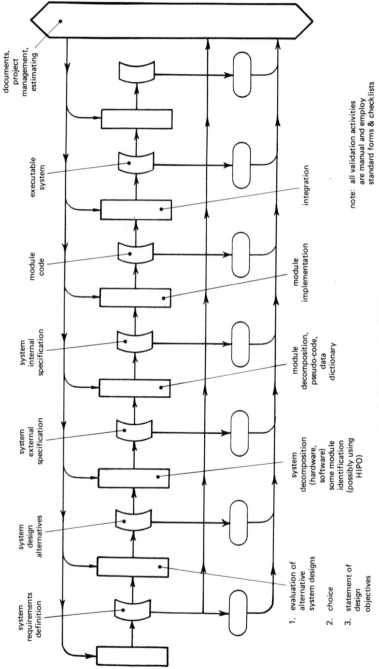

Figure 4   SDM/70 method (used by TESCI-Software)

control of documents, project management, estimating

executable system

module code

system internal specification

system external specification

system design alternatives

system requirements definition

integration

module implementation

module decomposition, pseudo-code, data dictionary

system decomposition (hardware, software) some module identification (possibly using HIPO)

1. evaluation of alternative system designs
2. choice
3. statement of design objectives

note: all validation activities are manual and employ standard forms & checklists

5   SDM/7Ø METHOD

The SDM/7Ø method [Atlantic Software (197Ø)], as used within TECSI-Software, is illustrated in Figure 4.

The SDM/7Ø method involves the development of several levels of specification prior to actual coding: an overall expression of requirements, a system specification and a set of module specifications. (In SDM/7Ø terminology these are known as the system requirements definition, the system external specifications and the system internal specifications). An interesting feature of the overall method is an activity which, following system requirements definition, explicitly considers a wide range of system design alternatives; these might include, for example, production of an entirely new system or use of commercially available packages.

The SDM/7Ø method provides guidelines for the individual life-cycle activities, and makes extensive use of standard forms and checklists both for the initial production of a particular specification and for the subsequent verification of the specification. Techniques such as HIPO charts and pseudo-code are employed within the SDM/7Ø framework, and a data dictionary is maintained for the emerging system.

Overall configuration control with SDM/7Ø is largely concerned with retaining control of the various levels of documents, and is integrated with the project management and estimating procedures.

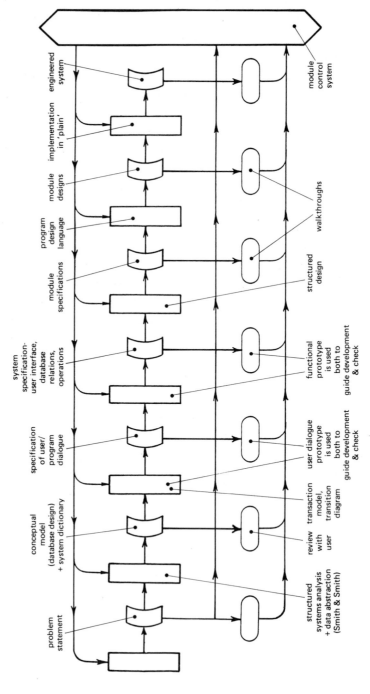

Figure 5 'Use' method (Wasserman, Medical Information Science (UCSF))

6 <u>USE METHOD</u>

The User Software Engineering (USE) Method [Wasserman (1981b)], developed at the Laboratory of Medical Science, University of California, San Francisico is shown in Figure 5. This method provides an interesting illustration of the benefits that can be obtained by optimising to one specific application area - in this case, that of interactive information systems.

The USE method combines two approaches which are normally regarded as being alternatives, rather than as being complementary, namely the early use of prototypes and the use of rigorous non-procedural specifications. The prototypes are used to obtain early feedback from the user, thereby increasing confidence that the system will actually do what the user wants. The functional prototype may also be employed to provide a temporary service to the user while the fully engineered system is developed.

The overall method is closely directed at the application area. Attention is therefore focused on the three key aspects of such systems: the user dialogue, the structure of the database, and the semantics of the operations which the user can invoke. User dialogues are specified by transition diagrams and a transition diagram interpreter provides rapid prototyping. Relational databases are employed, and the database structure is therefore specified as a set of relations. A database management system (Troll) is used both in prototypes and in engineered systems. Operations are specified by means of pre- and post-conditions specified in the first order predicate calculus, and also in natural language for the convenience of users rather than implementors.

Considerable attention has been paid to version and configuration control with the USE method, and a major tool of the method, the Module Control System [Wasserman et al (1981)], provides a high degree of automated support in this area.

Annex 5

Glossary of terms

This annex is written so that it may be read as an introduction to the terminology used in this report, as well as being used for reference purposes. Consequently the entries are not in alphabetical order, but in an order which is appropriate for the edification of an uninitiated reader!

APSE

APSE stands for Ada Programming Support Environment. An APSE is a system designed to support the development and maintenance of Ada applications software throughout its life cycle. The APSE is intended to be specifically oriented towards software for embedded computer applications. An APSE comprises a KAPSE and a set of software tools designed to support particular classes of application or particular methodologies. Typically APSE tools will be written in Ada.

KAPSE

KAPSE stands for Kernel Ada Programming Support Environment. The KASPE is the part of an APSE which provides database, communication and run-time facilities to support the execution of Ada programs, particularly APSE tools, and which provides a machine-independent interface to ensure the portability of tools between APSEs.

MAPSE

MAPSE stands for Minimal Ada Programming Support Environment. The MAPSE provides a minimal set of tools, written in Ada and supported by the KASPE, which are both

necessary and sufficient for the development and continuing
support of Ada programs. Clearly the MAPSE must contain at
least a text editor and an Ada compiler.

LIFE-CYCLE MODEL

A life-cycle model is a model of the full
lifetime of a system, from initial conception through to
final obsolescence. It should show the end products of the
system development, and show how these end products are
derived and verified. The model should also show how changes
to the system, both as consequences of design iterations,
and of post delivery maintenance, are controlled. The model
should cater for the simultaneous development, use and
maintenance of several versions of a system.

Typically life-cycle models describe the
life-cycle as a series of chronological phases. The
life-cycle model which we have adopted for this study is
based on the succession of representations produced during
the development of a system. Our model defines the methods
to be used in generating the representation, perhaps by a
transformation from an earlier representation, and in the
verification of the representation.

COHERENT OR INTEGRATED APSE

An APSE is coherent or integrated if it is based
on a set of methods which cover every aspect of system
development and maintenance according to a particular
interpretation of the life-cycle model. Specifically there
should be no gaps between the development methods - i.e.
there should be no part of the development process which has
to be pursued without the guidance of a particular method.
Similarly none of the methods should clash - i.e. should try
to guide the same part of the development in incompatible
ways. Finally the management methods should be capable of
controlling the development process as defined by the
development methods.

The concept of coherent methods is quite
similar, and is considered in detail in section 2.2.5.

REPRESENTATION

       A representation is a description of the system to be produced at some level of abstraction. Our life-cycle model is based on the assumption that it is necessary to produce a series of representations at different levels of abstraction in order to master the complexity of the system under development. The lowest level of representation will always be the system itself. When choosing a particular interpretation of the life-cycle model one is deciding which higher levels of abstraction one wishes to explicity represent and store within the APSE.

       In general a representation consists of objects, which may have a set of attributes each of which may take a set of values. There will also be relationships between these objects both within, and between, representations.

METHOD

       In our life-cycle model we use the term method to include the rules governing the transformation by which one representation is produced from another representation, and the rules by which the verification of certain properties of the representation can be accomplished.

       We exclude from our use of the term anything which is purely notational. Thus, in our terms, a method may employ a particular notation, and the procedure and notation may be inextricably linked, but the notation itself does not constitute a method.

METHODOLOGY

       Strictly methodology is the study or science of method. However we perpetrate the common misuse of the term by using "methodology" to mean the combination of methods produced to cover the whole software life cycle.

TRANSFORMATION

       The term transformation is used to mean the process by which a representation of a system is produced.

In general the transformation will be based both on existing representations and on other information, e.g. design decisions, not explicitly represented within the APSE database. In the case of the earliest representation, the requirements expression, the transformation will probably be based entirely on information not explicitly stored within the APSE. The rules for performing the transformation are defined by the method.

VERIFICATION

The verification of a representation is the operation of assessing certain properties of a representation and it's relationships to other representations. The verification procedure is defined by the method. Minimally the verification will be concerned with assessing the consistency and completeness of a representation, and with showing the accuracy of the transformation from the other representations as far as is possible.

CONSISTENCY AND COMPLETENESS

Consistency and completeness are, strictly speaking, separate concepts, but their definitions are sufficiently strongly related to justify defining them together. A representation is complete if it defines all the possible conjunctions of all the values of the objects in the representation. The possible conjunctions are defined by the relationships between the objects. Thus, for example, the definition of a function is complete if all the output values are specified for the whole range of all the input parameters.

A representation is consistent if no two parts of the representation are incompatible, i.e. if no two parts of the representation imply that an object must simultaneously hold more than one value. A representation cannot be shown to be (entirely) consistent if it is not complete, although it may, of course, be shown to be inconsistent even if it is not complete.

Consistency is also meaningful beween representations. Two representations are consistent if there are no incompatibilities between them given the relationships which exist between them. An obvious example of an incomapatibility would be where the specification for a procedure stated that it had four parameters, and in the implementation it had five.

PRODUCTION CONTEXT

The production context is the combination of all the factors that influence the way in which software is produced – such as the development organisation and the kind of programs that are to be developed. Two paradigms of production contexts were developed to guide the assessment of the methods, particularly the management methods. These paradigms are illustrated in Table 2.1 in section 2.5